EUROPEAN FUTURES

alternative scenarios for 2020

andrew duff and shirley williams

The Federal Trust for Education and Research

The Federal Trust's aim is to enlighten public debate on federal issues of national, continental and global government. It does this in the light of its statutes which state that it shall promote 'studies in the principles of international relations, international justice and supranational government.'

The Trust conducts enquiries, promotes seminars and conferences and publishes reports, books and teaching materials.

The Trust is the UK member of the Trans-European Policy Studies Association (TEPSA), a grouping of fifteen think tanks from Member States of the European Union.

Up-to-date information about the Federal Trust's publications and projects can be found at **www.fedtrust.co.uk**

© The Federal Trust for Education and Research 2001

ISBN 0 901573 63 9

The Federal Trust is a Registered Charity No. 272241
Dean Bradley House, 52 Horseferry Road,
London SW1P 2 AF
Company Limited by Guarantee No. 1269848

Marketing and distribution by Kogan Page Ltd
Printed by J W Arrowsmith Ltd

Contents

PART TWO

Preface

THIS BOOK saves you time, but it does not save you effort. It saves you time because it surveys many other scenarios exercises undertaken by governments, supranational and intergovernmental organisations, interest groups and think tanks, and gives you an overview of what Europe could look like in twenty years' time. But it does not save you effort because it makes you think. It makes you think because all the scenarios it offers are provocative. Like them or loathe them, they will cause you to sit up and think. Are these the futures we want? If so, which, and why?

Two authors penned this book, but over thirty thinkers contributed to it. They met in a study group organised by the Federal Trust over a period of a year or so, and came together in a conference that marked the culmination of that process. Here is a list of those who worked alongside the authors at some stage: Barbara Beck, Iain Begg, Graham Bishop, Richard Blackman, Tom Burke,

Vincent Cable, James Cornford, Harry Cowie, Ian Davidson, Michael Emerson, David Firnberg, Nigel Forman, Nigel Haigh, Alison Hook, Jonathan Hoffman, Charles Jenkins, John Kay, Giles Keating, Uwe Kitzinger, John Leech, John Lloyd, Peter Madden, Pauline Neville-Jones, Simon Nuttall, Liz Padmore, John Pinder, Jim Rollo, Bridget Rosewell, Paul Schulte, Susie Symes, Crispin Tickell and Stephen Tindale. The list may not be exhaustive as the process of consultation and refinement of ideas was prolonged, but all made their contribution, though the authors bear responsibility for the conclusions and the text put now before the reader.

The discussions of the group and the consultation of experts were facilitated by Rio Tinto plc, and the Federal Trust is pleased to acknowledge their generous support.

The Federal Trust is concerned to stimulate debate about good governance. This book does just that in making us think about what sort of European future we really want.

Martyn Bond
Director, The Federal Trust

european futures

andrew duff and shirley williams

PART ONE

Forces Shaping the Future of Europe

THE FEDERAL TRUST has been studying alternative scenarios for the future of Europe.[1] We have chosen the time frame of 2020, a period whose length encourages us to be conjectural and not entirely hypothetical, but whose relative shortness forces us to be both practical and responsible. Mindful that the next generation would properly blame us if we were to ignore the long-term implications of our present policies and strategies, we are seeking here to reach well beyond current preoccupations and obsessions.

We do not offer a cast-iron geographical definition of what we mean by 'Europe.' In one sense to be European is more a question of values than of nationality. We anticipate that the concept of 'Europe' will remain a subject of debate, but hope that any future disputes will be less about territory, both geographical and historical, and more about codes of ethics and systems of governance. Our alternative scenarios are intended to enlighten and stimulate debate.

Scenarios are not forecasts of the future. They tell stories about the future. They should be positive not normative. 'Might' rather than 'should' is the important distinction. The purpose of building scenarios is to challenge our mental maps of the future. Used well, scenarios can stimulate government and business to test their strategies, assess their preparedness, and even to adjust current policies to preempt, palliate or promote a particular outcome.

It is important to distinguish what we know from what we do not know. Some things are foreseeable, even if their impact may not be clear, such as demographic change and the depletion of natural resources. Other things are mysterious.

andrew duff and shirley williams

Among the forces that shape our future, some have strong internal dynamics of their own, such as capital market integration and the information technology revolution; others, for example the development of transnational constitutional liberalism or global climate change, may develop more slowly and may have a less immediate though no less significant effect on what is to come by 2020.

Part One of the report is concerned particularly with what forces may shape the future of Europe. On pages 47-55 we then try to assess the likely outcomes of these driving forces. Part Two builds our three alternative scenarios, plus a fourth which takes the form of a draft constitution for a federal union of European states and peoples. This is an example of what *might* happen. The postulated constitutional settlement *could* happen as a result of any of our three scenarios, although at different times and after different interim experiences.

The driving forces

Some of the more dynamic driving forces are to be found within Europe, spawned from Europe's own resources and exploiting its own potential. Today's Europeans may have only a tentative interest in, and limited control over, other external shaping factors, such as the emergence of the least developed countries. But the contemporary European stance of at best benign neglect towards developments in Africa, Latin America, India and, of course, China may well prove by 2020 to have been mistaken.

We seek to redress the great importance that inevitably attaches to 'government,' at various levels, by giving due consideration to the existence of other powerful actors, such as multinational business, the financial markets, the media, non-governmental organisations, organised religion and organised crime.

A perennial dynamic is the tension between Europe's core and its periphery; and much of what we have to say concerns the balance between integration on the one hand and, on the other, exclusion. Likewise, while we note (and welcome) the late re-emergence of a concept of European citizenship, we know that its less civilised, even barbarian alter ego of xenophobic nationalism has dominated much of the twentieth century and is still not expelled from Europe's shores.

All the driving forces and shaping factors are somehow linked in various ways. Some are second-wave, made up of economic and social reactions, often adverse, to earlier formative phenomena. How they all might interact with each other will fashion our alternative scenarios.

Economic and social integration

The European Union is an increasingly integrated economic entity, comprising fifteen member states and over 370 million people. It forms the largest economy in the world, accounting for over 20 per cent of world output. At the core of the EU is the euro-zone, the member states of the single currency area, initially with eleven member states: Austria, Belgium, Finland, France, Germany, Ireland, Italy, Luxembourg, the Netherlands, Portugal and Spain. Greece joined on 1 January 2001; others may follow. Europe's rates of growth and levels of employment are determined mainly by internal trade within the single market — comprising not only the fifteen current EU member states but also Switzerland, Norway and Iceland.

Each alternative scenario for the future of Europe depends in large measure on whether economic and social integration will bring about the sustained growth and fuller employment that is required over the long term to raise the overall quality and standard of life. Economic and Monetary Union (EMU) is the key.

In one way or another, by 2020 EMU will have profoundly transformed relations between the member states. If the plan original objectives have been achieved, the euro will by then have become a principal pillar, with the dollar, of the global monetary system. The euro will have delivered price stability and increased levels of long-term investment; it will have removed transaction costs and scotched currency speculation. Regions within the euro-zone will be competing with each other on the level playing field of the completed and consolidated single market. The institutions of the European Central Bank and Ecofin will have been accepted by public opinion and will be engaged with each other and European business in an enlightened dialogue. In such circumstances, people in 2020 will wonder how we ever used to cope with separate national currencies, and why the decision to introduce the euro had originally been so controversial.

Is it possible for EMU to be only a partial success? For example, EMU may work in the sense that it becomes a hard currency that attracts investment. But lack of provision to deal with its differential effects could lead to political turmoil in the poorer regions; and the European Central Bank might remain unloved. Alternatively, the high expectations surrounding the launch of the euro in 1999 may have been dashed by a series of shocks, such as the failure of Italy to tolerate a sustained programme of structural reform. Sterling's accession may never happen, and the euro would remain adopted only by the core member states at the heart of the Union. Those few states, dominated by Germany, are likely to have developed a tight form of federal relationship, managing what has become in effect a single economy with a centralised fiscal policy. But in such circumstances the outer tier of the Union languishes, the single market is weakened and the increased solidarity that was meant to mark the birth of the euro is dissipated.

Is it possible for EMU to collapse altogether, leading to a massive loss of confidence in the European project, renewed inflation, high unemployment, devaluation and to a widening disparity between core regions and the periphery? In these circumstances, even the single market would be in jeopardy. Protectionism would be inevitable and a resurgent nationalism tempting.

Demography

The economic development of Europe over the next twenty years will also be much affected by the ageing of society. According to Eurostat, the demographic trend will peak around 2020 when there will be about 390 million people in the current European Union of 15 member states. By then, the number of people under twenty years of age will have dropped by 7 million and the number of over-sixties will have risen by 24 million (and over-eighties by 9 million). According to the OECD, Italy's workforce will have shrunk by 15 per cent in 2020 and Germany's by 16 per cent, heralding thereafter a long period of low economic growth.

As in the USA today, the power of the elderly voter will not be able to be ignored. However, in terms of social welfare, a comparatively small number of taxpayers will have to support public education, social services and health care for many more non-wage earners.

On the other hand, there should be more job opportunities for fewer young people, requiring a higher overall level of skills and schooling. This creates a chance for European women to claim a larger share of the labour market — but only so long as child and elderly care provision is greatly enhanced.

Europe's labour shortages and the needs of working women will also lead naturally to a rise in immigration, especially of skilled workers and those in the childcare sector. Immigration, useful for the economy but generally feared and resented by resident populations, therefore confronts Europe's political leaders with one of their greater challenges. The effects of globalisation exacerbate popular resentment of newcomers, for globalisation tends to benefit the skilled and educated everywhere, but leaves in abeyance the uneducated poor, even in rich countries.

Traditionally, Europe's public welfare systems have been the popular link between the state and the citizen. Sharply rising medical and social security costs threaten the maintenance of this link. Social insurance is bound therefore to be privatised to some extent throughout European countries, although to varying degrees. Mandatory savings may be introduced in some states. As Europe's capital markets integrate, and financial services are liberalised, the citizen will learn to shop around for continuing education, health and life insurance policies, as well as mortgages and pensions. Such consumer agility will be especially marked in the euro-zone where competitive pressures will be at their most intense, and prices most transparent.

To what extent will European states retain minimum safety nets? In the USA some 17 per cent of the population is today uncovered by healthcare insurance. Europe's stronger social democratic tradition suggests a rather different approach. Unless there is a breakdown of social cohesion and civil society, the European electorate are unlikely to vote for the abandonment of collective provision. Even in the more individualist societies, education is the route to higher earnings and independence. Public education for 90 per cent of children is likely therefore to continue to be supported — and maybe even enhanced. In costly healthcare, however, the private sector might come to play more of a role. State provision may be more popular for those welfare functions that help society as a whole and also empower the individual. Public welfare to prop up the sick, unemployed and homeless may be less forthcoming.

Trade

The European Union's share of world trade in 2020 will be between 20 per cent and 35 per cent. (The UK Foreign Office suggests 25 per cent in 2010.) A big unknown is the pace and extent of the forthcoming enlargement of the European Union. At present the fifteen member states of the EU represent a $7.5 trillion economy, while the whole of East Europe only amounts to $300 billion. But growth rates will be higher in the East, especially in those states such as Poland, Hungary and the Czech Republic that are likely to be early new members of the Union. And these states will enjoy competitive exchange rates during their (presumably long) glide-path to membership of the euro-zone. The parenthesis is important. The euro, in the guise of its legacy currency the Deutsche Mark, is already in daily use in Kosovo and other parts of the EU's new imperium in the Balkans.

The evolution of the World Trade Organisation, and Europe's place within it, will be a key factor. An enlarged European Union enjoying sustained growth will be more likely to take the lead in building up the credibility of the WTO as the key factor behind an overall increase in global economic activity. Handled well, the WTO could develop its role as a norm-based, quasi-legal system and become a focal point for world government. Handled badly, a strong WTO would be an inflexible technocratic regulator damaging the prospects of less developed countries, and would run the risk of provoking a protectionist and nationalist backlash. America's stance is here pivotal.

Will the USA drive ahead to complete a free trade area of the Americas and the Pacific, leaving Europe with its own much smaller regional setting involving at best the Mediterranean and Black Africa, and maybe Russia and the Ukraine? If Russia and China have by then joined the WTO, as is likely, what are the consequences for the contemporary triad of Europe, Japan and the USA? India's potential as a driver of the non-European economy is probably assured so long as it can retain political stability. Although China will clearly have a very large domestic economy with a high savings ratio, the timing of its entry as a major trader in the global market place must be uncertain. On the other hand, a greater European economic space, including Russia and the Ukraine, must be a strong possibility, despite the attendant risk thereby of fostering the spread westwards of international, organised crime. Russia's current form of crony capitalism would be an impossible long-term partner for the West.

Indeed, the extent to which all previously oligarchic countries in the developing world open themselves to the liberalising effect of market forces is undoubtedly one of the major variables of the next two decades. Europe's contribution towards overseas development could be a key determinant of how well it is placed in the world prosperity league in 2020. Unless a more dedicated attempt is made by the rich countries to address global inequalities, markets will not expand and the poverty gap will grow not only in traditional sectors, like agriculture, but also in the new technologies that are vital for the development of the poorest communities on earth. Not many computers are being sold at the moment in Bangladesh, where the average worker would need to save all his wages for eight years to buy a standard PC. An imaginative programme to bridge the e-deficit (including the recycling of computers) coupled with systematic international debt relief would be helpful. The European Union could take much more of a lead in these matters than it has done to date within the appropriate forums such as the G8, IMF and the World Bank.

Europe's relative strength in the future also depends on the evolution of the currently faster-growing emerging economies. Brazil, China, India and Russia have huge growth potential but also massive social problems. Will Asian regional development flourish, or will Korea and the South East Asian countries flounder in corruption, social instability and environmental degradation? South-Eastern Asia (and Japan) have expanded over-rapidly: where they will be in 2020 depends in part on how they handle their present economic and democratic instability. Here the new process contained in the Asia-Europe Meetings (ASEM), and the overall richness of the Europe-Asia dialogue, is potentially important. Maybe the contemporary political crises in Indonesia, Malaysia and the Philippines will prove to be a catalyst for radical reform.

If emerging Asia chooses to develop in social democratic directions by shifting welfare functions from the community to the state, it will be unlikely to hold public sector spending down to current low levels or to continue to have such a competitive advantage in non-wage costs. The prospective development of these Asian countries may lie, by comparison, in building highly regulated and efficient regimes, such as Singapore today, or in encouraging specific high-tech sectors, as is the case with India.

Capital and labour

During the last twenty years, international transactions in bonds, equities and foreign exchange have increased much faster than trade. For example, the daily turnover of currency markets often exceeds the global stock of official foreign exchange reserves. Even today, the interdependence of world capital markets is enormous, and the onset of the euro has hastened the development of a single global market for capital, despite the somewhat nervous early stages of the new currency.

Where large, regionally integrated capital markets exist, such as in the United States, industry has a huge advantage. EU member states within the euro-zone will increasingly enjoy similar benefits. The Eurobond market was worth roughly $7000 billion on the creation of the euro in 1999; in the USA the bond market is already worth $10,000 billion. The growth of the euro Eurobond market is being very closely monitored by the so-called tiger economies of emerging Asia and Brazil and a big shift in portfolio investment from the dollar to the euro is anticipated.

Within the EU, it is to be expected that the euro will spawn transnational investment of pension and insurance funds, smashing artificial barriers, diversifying risk and encouraging a steady increase in the number of independent minded investors. This trend would be accentuated were the European Union to consolidate its single market and sharpen its competitive edge. At present, the necessary economic and structural reforms are being hampered by weak political leadership. Rhetoric outstrips action in capital market reform, transport, patents, energy supply and trade policy — with the result that the euro remains undervalued against the dollar. Successive meetings of the European Council have been trapped in a sterile debate between proponents of economic liberalism and adherents of state intervention.

Eventually it is possible that a new, Europe-wide consensus is reached on the design of a reformed social model that combines liberalisation, privatisation, tough competition and maximum entrepreneurial potential with a continuing respect for the role of the state and the social partners as arbiters in ensuring economic and social cohesion. Such a reformed European capitalism could continue to take somewhat different forms between member states, although just how different will depend not only on the political preferences of individual national governments, but also on the tolerance of European companies for variable geometry in the business environment.

It is, of course, wrong to assume that labour market 'flexibility' has to mean deregulation and the dismantlement of social services. Indeed, in the increasingly competitive environment, Europe will suffer badly if it ceases to value its workforce. One reason that German productivity is so high is that the substantional cost of social taxation has to be recouped by highly efficient management. Other member states have chosen to shift the burden of taxation away from labour towards other things, and to supplement low wages by family and tax credits. Diversity of culture and practice within the so-called European social model is huge, and is illustrated by the contrast between the UK on the one hand, where public expenditure is less than 40 per cent of GDP, and Sweden on the other, whose citizens are apparently content to have more than 60 per cent of their GDP spent by the state.

One might be surprised to see a growing reaction to the low level of employment in Europe, particularly in those countries, such as France, where governments are trying to restrict working time still further. At present only about 60 per cent of the employable EU population is in full-time work. We have already noted how demography will further reduce the size of the active European labour market.

Economic and Monetary Union imposes a very real constraint on national choice in the matter of levels of public expenditure, but as long as price stability and low public sector deficits are sustained throughout the euro-zone, there is no necessity to centralise fiscal policy at the EU level or to harmonise labour market practice across the member states. An unforeseen economic or political shock, however, (or more likely a series of them) could change the situation dramatically and impel member states to engage much more tightly in a common economic government. Needless to say, any decision to introduce common EU policy on payroll taxes, social security or unemployment benefit would predicate a much more radical leap towards a centralised federal state than is at present contemplated.

Civil society

One of the main features of a reformed European social model will be a widened and deepened 'social dialogue.' At present, government at the European and national level tends to limit its formal interlocutors to employers' organisations, trades unions and public enterprises. The representative capability of the conventional social partners at European level is limited, at least in respect of Europe's hundreds of thousands of small and medium-sized enterprises. The traditional social partners cover almost exclusively the world of formal employment. A growing number and proportion of Europe's citizens (particularly female) are retired, self-employed, part-time or home-workers. These economic actors are capable of networking transnationally without government. If the European dimension of economic and social democracy is to grow these sinews need to strengthen.

Functional partnerships might be developed between the EU institutions and regional and local authorities, which are legitimate and to an increasing extent autonomous players in the integrated European capital markets, and which also enjoy a significant role as informed or guided public purchasers in close touch with the citizen. The introduction of the euro will engender much tougher political and business competition between Europe's regions as the spread of credit is influenced by a plethora of matters other than the interest rate.

If trends in America are replicated, the already formidable presence of European non-governmental organisations will continue to grow. Social and economic interest groups are already agile transnationally, and add force to the concept of a pluralistic, multicultural European public space.

NGOs are more representative of the needs of many modern workers than the formal social partners. Pressure group NGOs for the elderly, the disabled or the impoverished, and utility user groups can no longer be ignored; their power is certain to increase as the voluntary and charitable sectors assume greater responsibilities as the traditional welfare state declines. More generally, NGOs serve to mobilise informed opinion and, like local government, help to articulate the choices of the pro-active consumer.

The British government, amongst others, argues that the European 'stakeholder society' may be a viable *via media* between libertarianism and communitarianism. In that case, European NGOs must be regarded, and regard themselves, as a formal and vital element in the new social partnership. Increasingly, they may also help actually to deliver social services under contract.

Knowledge and ethics

In an economic society where knowledge rather than mass labour is the key resource, European universities and research institutes have enhanced responsibilities. A successful university may see itself as a proponent of transnational, multicultural values, of high artistic and scientific standards, of equilibrium between innovation and conservation. The importance now attached by many universities to their role as regional actor is encouraging in this regard. The most enterprising are also conscious of their complementary duties in the European dimension.

Europe has a real problem to maintain the quality of its state systems of university education as public funding declines. Its higher education has been an important competitive factor, but is becoming relatively less outstanding at precisely the time when a greater premium than ever is put upon the production of a highly-skilled, multi-lingual élite as well as on leading edge science and technology innovation. Growing budgetary constraints force European universities to make invidious choices between the pursuit of sound learning on the one hand and the provision of an employment service on the other. Equipment standards and the comparative incomes of university research and teaching staff have declined. In consequence, few EU academic institutions are now regarded as internationally first rate. Greater differentiation can be expected between those universities that attract private finance from both students and business and those that cannot.

As the academic community rediscovers its common European antecedents dating back to the Renaissance and beyond, one may wonder why the Christian churches have been so muted in their response to European integration. In a transnational economic society where shared ethics are a source of direction and cohesion, Europe's religious communities have a realisable contribution to make. Although some churchmen in Central and Eastern Europe played a notable part in the collapse of the communist system, the stance of the official churches has been more socially conservative than reformist. The ecumenical forces within Protestantism, Catholicism and Orthodoxy have yet to participate in a meaningful way in the building of the new Europe.

Management and participation

The great economic potential of postnational European society raises questions about the state of its corporate management. Again influenced by contemporary trends in America, competitive firms in the future globalised environment are likely to be larger but also more decentralised than at present. Some may adopt a highly participative management style within a federal framework. In a reformist scenario, worker participation within companies may come to replicate the highly participative culture of civil society at large.

A growth in voluntary and part-time work, non-wage remuneration and even the monetisation of domestic chores and the concept of 'time dollars,' break down traditional barriers between labour and non-labour. In these circumstances, retirement age would become fluid or even abolished altogether. Tax regimes would become more flexible, with integrated income tax and welfare systems. Freedom of information, data and consumer protection policies would be much more salient. Education and training opportunities would have to be made available throughout working lives, and regular, anticipated periods out of full-time employment may have to be supported by new-style, tripartite contracts between individual, company and state.

In Europe, at least, such cooperative arrangements could only be sustainable to the mutual benefit of all concerned if an individual had an obligation to up-grade his or her skills, reflected, in turn, in patterns of remuneration. In any case, old definitions of structural unemployment may be dispensed with, just as nominal shareholder control of companies might be out-moded.

Migration

A strong determinant of the future economic development of Europe is labour mobility. An immobile workforce would be an impediment to making a success of Economic and Monetary Union. How successful may we expect the European Union to be in making a reality of freedom of movement of people?

As we have seen already, demographic changes and labour market rigidities within Europe will lead to a growing demand for immigration from outside the Union of both skilled and unskilled workers. Should Europe prove to be a rare haven of freedom, prosperity and justice within a turbulent world, the supply of migrant workers as well as refugees will increase. The political problem is that the more permissive Europe is about internal migration, the more hostile its domestic opinion is likely to be to immigration. It is a paradox that the more open and participative European society becomes, the more difficult we may find it to deal sensibly with outsiders. Greater liberalisation requires heavy policing, closer judicial cooperation and deeper political trust between member states of the Union and their peoples.

The question of migrant labour is one of the most difficult issues confronted by the EU and the candidate countries in the present round of enlargement negotiations. How the question is resolved has huge consequences not only for Europe's economic development and both internal and external security, but also for our moral integrity. The privilege of European Union citizenship is indivisible: either it applies to all nationals of all member states or it is a figment. The Charter of Fundamental Rights of the European Union, solemnly proclaimed at Nice in December 2000, is insistent on this point.

Imaginative policies are now needed to help the social development of countries at the frayed edge of the Union, wherever that may prove in the end to be. Compensatory investment by EU banks and firms within neighbouring countries — the export of jobs rather than the import of labour — may be part of the answer. But that implies a high degree of stability, profitability and openness. A strategic commitment by the Union to the economic development of its near-abroad would involve a common and progressive approach to the problems of education, debt relief and public health; and it may result in the spreading of European norms about civil society and environmental protection to the whole neighbourhood. At this stage, it is not easy to be sanguine about the capacity either of the European Union to deliver such a package, or of its neighbours to receive it. At some stage, however, there must be the likelihood of a concerted effort to develop a pan-European consensus on all these matters as the fruit of a greatly improved relationship between the European Union, Russia, Turkey and the Maghreb. Intensified cooperation over the environment, infrastructure and fundamental rights may hold the key, although the question of immigration from the South and East towards Western Europe cannot be ducked.

Infrastructure

The EU has established plans for ambitious Trans-European Networks (TENs) in transport, energy and telecommunications. These, if realised, will provide a state-of-the-art infrastructure for a competitive and integrated European economy, and need not be confined to the formal borders of the Union. Nor need they be publicly owned and operated, as in the past. Indeed, the key to the development of TENs may be to build effective public-private partnerships for the design, financing and management of the networks, and this requires not only a cultural change but also the transnational liberalisation of pension and insurance funds in order to generate sufficient investment. How successful will relatively limited public funds be in leveraging private money? Pension reform, therefore, is clearly crucial. The pace of European capital market integration is a key determinant here, and will be much affected by the success of EMU.

A more competitive Europe will demand and require less congested transport systems and more interconnectable, networked services. Europe's public utilities, which are at present still characterised by national monopolies, will suffer low growth, high costs and continued fragmentation unless universal service obligations can be reconciled with the advance of liberalisation and privatisation. Alternatively, by 2020, environmental imperatives may have created the need for a fully integrated and publicly subsidised pan-European transport or water system. And all forms of communications may be subject to taxation at saturation points, including congestion of motor cars and of megabytes. North West Europe already seems full up. Within the travel-to-work area formed roughly by Manchester, Paris and Hamburg, the private car journey will surely become more exceptional by 2020 and the use of public transport the norm.

Technology

It is difficult to grasp the pace and scope of the information technology revolution. Today, the processing power of a microchip doubles roughly every eighteen months; and its cost halves every two years. Of all the scientists that ever lived, over 90 per cent are living now.[2]

But in exploiting information technology Europe lags behind. By 2010, Japan will have connected all businesses and households to an interactive, multimedia, broadband, fibre-optic system. In the United States, the cost of using the internet is already fixed as part of the basic telecoms service, and 35 per cent of American homes have PCs compared with 10 per cent in the EU (20 per cent in the UK).

The new industrial revolution will be generated in part by competition between clusters of innovation centres in different parts of the world. This is an obvious feature of the digital and biogenetic technologies, but also of the older industries, such as steel, where Europe may succumb entirely to the more competitive products of India and the Pacific Rim. Later, low wage but highly skilled groups in China might beat South East Asia in the field of leading edge software technology.

On the other hand, information technology makes all parts of the world more accessible and, potentially, networkable. The prospect of a global 'wired boom' should not be discounted, and it may be the evolution of self-organising networks which takes us by surprise in 2020. Photonics will be replacing silicon technology, with significant energy savings in train.

The social and economic consequences of this information revolution are difficult to gauge. The success of e-commerce depends upon the provision of universal access to the internet and a trustworthy, global regulatory system for data protection, taxation regime and legal contract. Basic education will need to spread far and fast before the world's human resources can be used more creatively. Will Europeans have the wit to take a lead?

The planet

For the past decade, the total human population has been increasing at the historically unprecedented rate of 2 per cent per annum. Although this rate may fall to 1.5 per cent by 2020, and further thereafter, the population explosion is perhaps the most blatant and unmalleable of our shaping factors. The total world population will have grown from 6 billion now to 8 billion in 2025 and to 10 billion by 2050. This is uncontestably dramatic — especially when seen from a Europe whose own population is shrinking.

At the same time, the planet's climate is changing. Although there is still dispute about the detailed science, the broad contention is now accepted that, first, rapid climatic change is disruptive and potentially catastrophic and that, second, mankind is largely responsible for precipitating the change. It follows, third, that what is done can at least partially be undone, although a broad political consensus has still to be developed in order to accomplish a radical modification in social and industrial behaviour.

In December 1997, for example, the United Nations' conference in Kyoto committed all developed states to a 6 per cent reduction in greenhouse gases below 1990 levels by 2012. The EU agreed to a reduction target of 8 per cent; the USA to 7 per cent and Japan to 6 per cent. All countries except for the US are struggling to meet these targets.

The effect of the planet's climate change on Europe is likely to make it less temperate. Food and water supply will have to adapt. Modest changes in moisture and temperature have enormous implications for pathogenic micro-organisms; the development of new diseases and the resurgence of old may be confidently expected. Already, the failure of antibiotics to destroy mutated viruses plus the erosion of public health systems in, for example, Algeria, Russia and the Ukraine is very serious.

The AIDS epidemic rages in the developing world, reversing what gains there have been in public health in recent decades. By the 2020s, AIDS will be the biggest killer in Sub-Saharan Africa, reducing life expectancy to as low as 40 years in some countries. Asia is very much at risk: already four million Indians and five million Chinese are HIV-positive. If a cure to AIDS has been discovered by 2020, it may only be affordable by rich countries unless the pharmaceutical companies can be made to loosen their grip on the production of generic drugs.

The combination of the effects of population explosion, disease and climate change may provoke a world refugee crisis of an awesome scale as well as large-scale domestic challenges in the fields of public health and food security. Safe-haven Europe will not be insulated from these problems. It may have to choose between a Fortress Europe attitude sacrificing traditional liberal values or a marked increase in financial support to enable poor countries to develop faster. The current controversy over genetically modified agriculture is another good example of the ethical and scientific conflicts yet to be resolved.

Environmental survival allows of no short-term solutions. The problems are long-term and transnational; this generation's efforts to tackle them will benefit only the next generation, separated by time and, often, space. What is required of us, therefore, is an impressive, concerted and radical act of political will. The European Union may or may not confront this somehow.

There is a sense in which Europe's environmental politics during the last twenty five years have been accorded a fairly easy agenda. The main first generation issues have been noise pollution, the quality of sea, river and drinking water, waste management, recycling and radioactivity. Public concern was fairly high; government regulation at EU and member state level was appropriate; and the economic cost to business was modest.

Nowhere is the new environmental agenda more testing than in securing safe supplies of hygienic food and clean water. The role of biotechnology may be crucial in this regard, and much is bound to depend on the European science effort in this field.

The European Union has made a respectable effort to combat pollution; it has developed and tested policy tools; it has defined its policy objectives; and, increasingly, it has designed well-honed measurement indicators. The EU now has an escalating responsibility to clean up the degraded environment of the applicant states from Central and Eastern Europe. Environment policy is central to the enlargement process; but it has also become clear that the applicant states will be unable to catch up with Western environmental standards without significant and long-term investment from the EU.

Enlargement is only one indicator that, in the next twenty five years, the EU's duty to the environment will deepen. This second generation of issues concerns climate change, biodiversity and biotechnology. They will relate more directly and more drastically to the global economy. Billions of people and whole regions may be affected by famine, drought and disease. The wilful or accidental spoliation of forests, oceans or croplands is more than an environmental nuisance. If at some point their degradation were to become irreversible, the eco-system would be destroyed. That would be cataclysm.

Sustainable development

The European Union has made great efforts to understand and to embrace the concept of sustainable development. The Treaty of Amsterdam (1997) prescribes that environmental policy shall be integrated across the spectrum of the activities of the Union (Article 6 TEC). But the conservation of natural resources requires hefty persuasion and robust collaboration. Public opinion and business tend to resist the radical re-structuring of markets, especially with regard to the use of the private motor car. Will the European Union be successful in devising a comprehensive programme of environmental measures with the strategic objective of sustainable development but with enough local content and simple cost benefits (as in curbing traffic congestion) to appeal to the citizen?

Surveys suggest that public opinion strongly identifies the environment (with defence) as a popular reason for building Europe. But this honourable sentiment may only be properly tested once the EU reaches agreement on the introduction of environmental taxation and advances the more radical reform of the common farm and fisheries policies. Frustrated with slow progress in these directions on an EU-wide basis, certain member states may want to go faster and further than others in developing environmental policy under the terms of the 'flexibility' clauses of the Amsterdam Treaty (as modified at Nice). More demanding environmental standards by the EU's economically most advanced states can be embraced, but only if they are not so discrepant as to pose insurmountable challenges to the integrity of the single market, or begin to distinguish sharply between first and second class member states. Such entrenched differentiation might turn out to be highly unpopular.

The participative Europe of the reformed social model would continue to spawn environmentalist NGOs, regional and local authorities and even companies to press for strong ecological policies, both at home and abroad. However, popular participation could backfire to frustrate the best laid plans of environment strategists. Media attention focused on motorway or airport developments or on nuclear waste disposal may provoke mass popular demonstrations. Significant changes in party political support induced by major controversies — for example, the introduction of carbon energy taxes or legislation on genetic engineering — may result in political instability, in which case perseverance with the necessary long-term environment strategies becomes ever more problematical.

The European Commission would be strongly backed by the European Parliament in pursuit of a high profile for environmental diplomacy in the Union's international trade negotiations. It is possible that public support for tough environmental policies at home would be kindled by a hostile reaction to the poor record of other countries, such as the United States or China, in controlling their greenhouse gas emissions. This would give the Union a chance to play the green card in world affairs, possibly by launching an initiative to establish a global community for sustainable development, initiated by a group of democracies prepared to accept the new community's rule of law with respect to emissions that lead to global warming.[3] The Union would thereby be elevating environmental policy to be, after peace and prosperity, its third raison d'être. This might transform the way Europeans see their own future, as well as the Union's place in the general scheme of things. It should also encourage the wider spread of liberal democracy, eventually worldwide.

Fundamental rights

There is a close connection between the pursuit of environmental policy objectives and the promotion of human rights. Both have their interdependent domestic and international contexts. Both are areas in which the European Union could make a special, distinctive contribution popular with public opinion. And well-crafted initiatives in both fields might be expected to recruit other liberal democracies to support an enhanced role for the EU on the world stage.

Again, the Treaty of Amsterdam has helped. First, it consolidated the foundation of the EU itself on the principles of liberty, democracy, respect for human rights and the rule of law (Article 6 TEU). Second, it introduced a clause to allow for membership of the Union to be suspended in the case of a 'serious and persistent breach' of human rights (Article 7 TEU). Third, it empowered the Union to 'take appropriate action to combat discrimination based on sex, racial or ethnic origin, religion or belief, disability, age or sexual orientation' (Article 13 TEC). Fourth, it opened up the prospect of developing a common judicial 'area of freedom, security and justice' corralled by a common immigration and asylum policy.

The fresh emphasis on fundamental rights has been taken forward by the drafting and proclamation of the EU Charter of Fundamental Rights in 2000. The Charter sets out as clearly as possible how the individual stands in relation to the Union. It draws on the classical human rights established by the Council of Europe after 1945, but codifies more modern rights drawn from the EU Treaties and the *acquis communautaire*, including economic and social rights, the right to good administration, freedom of information and sustainable development. Its focus is the European Union, and many want the Charter to be made fully binding upon the Union's institutions and agencies, so that individual citizens will be able to seek redress in the Court of Justice at Luxembourg for alleged abuses of power.[4] In parallel with these developments, the EU needs to clarify its relationship with the Council of Europe and consider whether the Union itself should sign up to the European Convention on Human Rights (ECHR).

External security

Braced by this new self-assurance in the field of fundamental rights, the Union has strengthened its own profile for the benefit of both present and prospective members. It is also better placed to justify its increasing role in foreign, security and defence policy, a role which may be stimulated fast by the establishment of a truly EU armed force, of which the new Rapid Reaction Force may be a precursor. The assumption of a military dimension to the activities of the Union will have very important consequences for European integration, and these are starkly illustrated in our alternative scenarios. Whatever happens, it will be essential for the Union to remember that its primary goals of economic development, a safe and clean environment and good, democratic government could not be met in violent or warlike conditions.

Yet the threat of conflict will be ever present for the Union, however peaceable its intentions. The growing threats will be both external and internal, and will have connections. And there are almost bound to be unknowable events, possibly spurred by environmental disasters like Chernobyl, as well as provoked by new world leaders of an eccentric, deranged or volatile type.

Europe's near-abroad has a number of clearly discernible areas of potential conflict. The intractable politics of the Balkans and the Middle East are already with us. EU enlargement portends great changes to the foreign and security stance of the Union. Cypriot membership, pre-eminently, will be a complex proposition, given Turkey's position in Nato. Developments in the Maghreb are also likely to become critical during our scenario period.

Further afield, Europe's relations with China will be a strong determining factor. The Chinese are concerned about US proposals for missile defence. Russians are worried about the security of their porous frontier with China: already about five million Chinese have crossed it illegally. Europe could be in a position to ease potential conflicts and to promote peaceful outcomes.

The lingering colonial ties and often poignant imperial legacies of several European states may yet prove troublesome, particularly in Africa for which the next two decades are likely to be especially unstable and where European paternalism is still resented.

The EU may well be drawn into neighbourhood disputes in Africa in order to pursue humanitarian objectives or to try to limit military escalation. To the East, it would be difficult for Nato and the European Union to remain indifferent to fighting between the former republics of the Soviet Union, wars which may threaten to unlock nuclear arsenals. Disputes over oil, gas or water as well as ethnic and religious strife could trigger military action in the Ukraine, the Caucasus or Central Asia.

Corrupted, hollow states, where the rule of law, public health, public administration and internal security have broken down, may proliferate. Already, Algeria, the Ukraine, Moldova, and Belarus share most of those characteristics. In others, as in the Balkans or Turkey, rebellion and civil war may create a vacuum which the European Union, for fear of something worse, must fill. Political instability or international terrorism might also suck Europe into Trans-Caucasian embroilment.

Europe-Asia

At either end of the northern land mass, two new world powers are emerging. One is an enlarged European Union. The other is Asian, where the dominant power has been Japan but is likely to be China. The quality of the developing relationship between these two different entities will be a powerful determinant of future global politics and economics. A strong Europe-Asia relationship would have much to contribute to building with the USA a more balanced global order. Europe's direct investment in Asia is lagging behind that of the US, and could be raised. Europe's social and cultural traditions, deployed with tact, could be highly beneficial influences upon the transition of Asia. The EU would be wise to observe the cardinal principles of consistency and reciprocity to govern its human rights policy. Then one may expect to see a steady improvement in the application throughout Asia of universal human rights, a general rise in social and economic conditions, and the growth of democracy.

Asia faces enormous environmental degradation, with which it cannot cope left to its own devices. A partnership of European government and industry would help emerging Asia plug the gap between investment which is cheap and dirty and that which constitutes sustainable development. In this context, the EU's experience in Eastern Europe is helpful. Additional financing mechanisms, training, and the transfer of technological and management know-how would be needed. In both the environmental field and in fast-growing telecommunications, European participation in Asia would be vital to Europe's own employment and prosperity.

Europe-Russia

One thing of which we may be absolutely certain is that the European Union will spend a lot of time and energy watching and analysing developments in Russia. Several alternative futures are themselves suggested by members of the Duma.

Russia may choose to modernise itself on the basis of its European traditions, rightly expecting to be encouraged in this process by Nato and the EU. Or it may move atavistically to challenge the West by incursions into Belarus, Moldova and the Ukraine. Or it may prefer to find new partners to the South and East, in Iran, Iraq and China — as well as trying to resurrect a new politico-military entity in the former Soviet states in Asia and also Afghanistan. Such a nineteenth century course could revive the historic destabilisation of the Indian sub-continent.

Alternatively, Russia may fail to make a decisive choice in any direction, lurching between reformation and reaction at home, and ceasing to be a major player in the international system. It is likely, however, that the discovery of Russia's true security community will lie somewhere at the end of a process of radical domestic reform. In that case, for Europe and Nato to collude with the powerful forces of inertia within the Russian military might prove to be a terrible mistake. Effective instruments for developing a dynamic security partnership between Europe and Russia, if they do not already exist, must be developed.

Europe-America

The key to how Europe copes with its future external security must be the transatlantic partnership. In the past, US encouragement for European integration has been of critical importance. In the future, a successfully enlarged and more self-confident EU may be less reliant on American support. And American support for Europe-building may in any case be less forthcoming as the axis of American politics shifts from the Atlantic to the Pacific.

Certainly the loyalty of European public opinion to America should not be presumed. Tensions may emerge, perhaps over environmental or libertarian issues. European disaffection with America was a considerable factor at the time of the Vietnam War, and renewed European hostility to US military power may be triggered by technological adventurism, of which National Missile Defence may be an example, or the opening of a new chapter in imperial misadventures, such as Somalia or Columbia. By 2020, for a variety of reasons, the long-suffering Yanks might finally have gone home.

Early decisions will have to be taken about Nato's future. The Alliance has already enlarged to include Poland, the Czech Republic and Hungary, but adding new members is not a seminal part of the Nato process; and in any event — because for all Europe to join would be a fair nonsense — Nato enlargement is likely only ever to be one element in developing greater stability for all Europe. What really matters is the projection of the transatlantic security umbrella and the spread of burden sharing, as well as the effect of all this on Russia. The Euro-Atlantic Partnership Council (EAPC) comprising the 19 Nato members and 25 other states, formed in 1997, may be the forum with a future, leading in time to a radical transformation of Nato from the traditional military alliance into world police force. The express intention is to transcend former enmities, and the art of practical collaboration between armies is already being learned in Partnership for Peace.

Might there be two Natos? The first would be the inner core bound by cast-iron Article 5 guarantees of mutual defence, maintaining an expensive and integrated military machine capable of low to high intensity operations; it would need a streamlined and more mobile command structure. (France may or may not have become an orthodox player.) The second Nato would work to limit Western military involvement in a crisis, emphasising conflict resolution and peace-keeping. It would depend more on joint training and the integration of staff officers. Under EAPC auspices, there could be regional examples of reinforced cooperation.

The Bosnian War (1993-95) and Kosovan War in 1999 tested the European military pillar of Nato nearly to destruction. It was proven beyond reasonable doubt that the West Europeans could not act alone without the Americans. This sobering experience spurred the European Union into action, and in December 1999 the European Council established a Headline Goal in terms of EU military capabilities for crisis management operations. The aim is to enable the Union to deploy, by the year 2003, and sustain for at least one year, military forces of up to 60,000 troops to undertake the full range of the so-called Petersberg tasks set out in the Amsterdam Treaty. These consist of humanitarian and rescue tasks, peacekeeping, and crisis management, including 'peacemaking.' The role of the new Rapid Reaction Force will be to undertake military operations led by the EU in response to international crises, in circumstances where Nato as a whole is not engaged militarily. In addition, the EU decided to create a permanent political and military structure, including a Political and Security Committee, a Military Committee and a Military Staff. Everyone is at pains to insist that these dramatic initiatives do not imply the creation of a European army — but, of course, one day they may do.

It is obvious that Americans and Europeans together need to concert their views about the future political and territorial stretch of the Atlantic Alliance. In the past, coordination between Nato and the EU, both Brussels-based organisations each with a majority of joint members, has been extraordinarily poor.

If a coherent European security and defence identity is to emerge, and if Europe is to make a major contribution to the maintenance of peace and the rule of law, the Union will need to have obtained the active consent of the United Nations. In these circumstances, reform, and possibly even the salvation, of the United Nations might become a top priority of the Union.

For the Euro-American defence partnership to survive, it will need to rest upon a sensible division of labour between European soft power and US technological might. The alternative, naturally, is for the existing security arrangements to stagger on, a source of endless political anxiety, low military capability and rising cost. But this is hardly an attractive proposition, especially for the Europeans who, unlike the Americans, cannot walk out on Europe.

Where an international crisis is of such significance that it demands military intervention by Nato, including the United States, a new problem may well rise. The Bush administration's review of American military capabilities may well lead to a new emphasis on intelligence gathering and advanced information technology instead of the heavy conventional resources of the past. Until now, the EU, with the exception of the United Kingdom, has not been fully integrated into American intelligence and information gathering systems. It is unlikely that Congress would agree to the complete integration of the EU into the US network, even if this were to be sought by the Europeans.

Internal security

Long-term investors want to know how stable European society will be in 2020. The continued growth of the middle class suggests that large-scale, mass violence is unlikely, although even among affluent young people resentment at the scale, distance and technocratic character of government and global inequities, often articulated through environmental protest, may be a continuing trend. We are already witnessing an overall decline in civility, peppered with occasional outbursts of remonstrative violence, for example at the WTO talks in Seattle or the EU Summit in Gothenburg. The globalisation of the disgruntled is already evident on the internet which can be, if misused, a vicious weapon.

Particular elements are certain to be disaffected or aggrieved. Terrorism, often organised internationally, is surely to be a permanent feature of European life, and is in some respects the obverse of European humanitarianism. Motivations for violence may be ethnic, religious, criminal, separatist or radical. Some terrorism will be provoked by conflicts external to the EU, such as those of the Palestinians, Kashmiris, Sikhs or Kurds. Other terrorists, like the IRA, ETA or the Corsican separatists, are indigenous and, gloomily, tend to be self-perpetuating.

Even without the Balkans, enlargement may introduce to the Union new member states that prove to be more volatile and less urbane than its western core. European integration itself may provoke a nationalist or racist backlash in some quarters, especially if it is closely associated in the popular mind with the adverse effect of globalisation on an impoverished and ill-educated under-class. Serious privation in Eastern Europe outside the capital regions may fuel disintegration and crime. Unless Russia, in particular, succeeds in establishing the machinery and integrity of civil order it will remain a potent source of dangerous criminality.

Law and order

Changing technology will throw up new ways to be violent — and new methods to cope with violence. New technology used by the state to combat violence may also test the limit of civil liberty. The protection of individual human rights is the critical antithesis to sophisticated policing and state surveillance, and a binding EU Charter of Fundamental Rights would be a valuable safeguard.

Europol has the potential to develop into a European FBI, although the reconciliation of supranational with local police forces would require a very much stronger political system and proper democratic accountability, with vital in-built checks and balances, than the Union presently enjoys. At the moment, democratic scrutiny is at its weakest at the EU level in the field of police and judicial cooperation in criminal matters.

The Treaty of Amsterdam made some notable advances in rationalising how the Union deals with its interior affairs, including the gradual incorporation of the Schengen Agreement. Progress on a common asylum and immigration policy is envisaged by 2003. Relevant jurisprudence from the European Court of Justice can be anticipated, especially if the new Charter of Fundamental Rights is made mandatory.

Once the European Union has established a superior fundamental rights regime, and following its enlargement to include most of the present members of the Council of Europe, the future of the European Court of Human Rights in Strasbourg is more difficult to fathom. Nevertheless, some pan-European judicial arm, similar to that of the Council of Europe, will still be required to oversee and encourage the development of civil liberties in those states, such as Russia, which either do not aspire to EU membership or do not meet the criteria.

One heavy cost of globalisation and EU enlagement will be better organised and more ruthless international crime, exploiting weaknesses in public authority. The challenge of transnational crime may drive Europe back into defensive (and oppressive) national redoubts, were the integrated approach to fail. Or it may spawn imaginative common legal, political and policing responses, the outcome of which is the formation of a new moral consensus committed to social justice and conflict prevention and resolution. This would require a determined effort by the Union to build a wide European public space and to develop an inclusive concept of European citizenship.

A new European enlightenment, based on civic education, social dialogue, and effective leadership is not impossible, but it would require a common commitment that is still sadly distant.

Governance

Given the complexity and volume of the challenges it faces, postnational Europe needs a sustained period of exceptionally good government. The design of its institutions and policy instruments at all levels of government, as well as the social values that underpin them, are important. The distances between the emerging supranational institutions and the public they serve, as well as the lack of openness and clarity surrounding many of their activities, accentuates the need for a continuing period of political reform.

As far as values are concerned, we would highlight a question which we find raised implicitly by our discussion of the driving forces behind European integration. We expect Europe to eschew both radical libertarianism on the one hand and conservative communitarianism on the other. So will Europe discover a third way comprising a more participative but market-oriented society and a high level of social cohesion modifying economic inequality? A key determinant is the size of public expenditure.

At the start of the twentieth century government spending in the industrialised countries accounted for less than one-tenth of national income. At the start of the twenty-first century, public spending amounts for just less than half of GNP. Even radical free-market reformers, like Margaret Thatcher, have been unable to reverse the trend in Europe. The size of government, and its distance from the people it serves, has expanded not only to fight Europe's wars in the first half of the century but also to cope with the task of reconstruction in the second half. Armed forces and social welfare, including public health care, take the two biggest slices of public expenditure, and, despite liberalisation and increased emphasis on private insurances, are set to continue to do so. Although there are undoubted economies of scale for industry, European integration does not come cheap for government.

Within the context of bigger, post-national governance, the role and status of global corporations are fundamental to the changing nature of the relationship between government and the citizen. These corporations are already huge, especially in the information technology sector. The market capitalisation of Microsoft outstrips the gross national product of Canada; the size of Vodafone is equivalent to the GNPs of Denmark, Finland and the Czech Republic combined; Nokia alone is valued at more than twice the GDP of its home country, Finland.[5] Faced with these corporate giants, is it too much to hope that state authorities might grow to be more self-effacing, and even less pretentious in the claims they make on the citizen?

What may be required is a style of central government which is less obviously interfering. The autonomy of regional and local governors, however, can only be realised effectively if EU and national regulations are both clear about the intention of legislation and suitably permissive about how policy may be implemented on the ground. Again, the EU Charter of Fundamental Rights is a useful tool in this respect, setting out the principles of democracy and the rule of law along with contemporary norms of good and open government, and of high standards in social, economic and ecological policies. The Charter could stimulate a new understanding of the principle of subsidiarity, not only in geographical but also in functional terms, concentrating on the role of the citizen in a federal society.

European democratic society of the twenty-first century might be one in which the capacity of the individual for political self-expression is enhanced. Electoral and institutional reform may be undertaken in many states and at the EU level in order to develop a system which reflects the pluralism of modern society, the increasing autonomy of the citizen-elector and the rights of minorities to fair representation. Increased use of referenda, citizens' juries and focus groups may be anticipated. This in turn will encourage the involvement of special interest groups, which, in America, are powerful enough to swamp exercises in direct democracy. Innovative consultative methods may proliferate, and may begin at an earlier stage in policy formation than is traditional, at least in Britain.

But a key issue will be who controls the agenda of the media and poses the political questions. Globalised, multi-media power is bound to expand exponentially. Political opinion as well as consumption patterns will surely be easier to mobilise and change than ever before. Europe has an important cultural choice to make between managed or spontaneous participation. EU competition policy, within the WTO regime, could be made to bite effectively on the multi-media industry. National preference or cultural singularity will nonetheless be under continuing pressure to conform to globalised, US-led norms.

The digital revolution is creating big new opportunities for on-line, multi-media, interactive communication. The World Wide Web is readily available via computers to any commercial interest or political lobby now. As soon as the internet is available via cable on digital TV screens rather than computers its use will multiply. Shopping, *e-commerce*, is first; but opinion pollsters, policy-led opinion formers and the academic community are not far behind. Faced with this plethora of information, how the public discriminates and deliberates is uncertain. Virtual political communities are unlikely to be as binding as the traditional public meeting in the village hall, and the fall in voter participation may already reflect the rise of *e-politics*. Undoubtedly, the increase in impersonal contact resulting from the internet has implications for individual, social and sexual morality.

The web is essentially an American-English language medium. Other European languages will struggle to compete with or compensate for the predominance of English as the global network language. The question of language and cultural differentiation is already and will continue to be sensitive for Europeans as they pursue a common identity. How diverse that identity will be depends in part on how open European governments are prepared to be in making information freely available. They should follow the American example, at least in this respect. Let the people decide.

Conventional political parties find this information revolution rather problematical. A more freethinking style of politics is the consequence of the end of hierarchical structures and the explosion of available information. The challenge of supranational politics defies the political party founded to seek office in one nation state. This pattern is mirrored in the world of work, where traditional trades unions become less suitable vehicles of labour participation and cease to fulfil their historical, integrating function. And it is reflected, too, in the relative decline of the church. A looser, more diverse, more pluralistic civil society is striving to assert herself. The rise of NGOs means a broadening of the social dialogue. Many of them already surf national borders, have established direct working relations with supranational institutions, and are well versed in working around the back of national government. The contrast with the old, national political parties could not be more stark.

NGOs will certainly play a vital if ambivalent role in shaping future decision-making. They should help to create functional democratic communities as a legitimate counter to government. Yet they could also become obsessional minorities. How such functional communities will live in harmony with the political elite is not clear. Will there one day be a move to regulate NGOs?

The European Union

The existence of the European Community – now Union – already challenges traditional notions of state sovereignty in Western Europe. We would prefer to see the EU develop into a federal union of states and peoples, with the states represented powerfully in the Council and the peoples represented just as powerfully in the European Parliament, with the European Commission as a strong and accountable executive. We believe that that basic structure is best suited to specifically European requirements and can provide good government for our complex, diffident, postnational Europe. We fully recognise, however, that many others would wish to revert to more traditional concepts of state organisation and would seek to reduce the power of the European Commission, Parliament and Court of Justice in favour of the Council and of member state parliaments. There are even some who would prefer to see the dismantling of the Union altogether.

EU-30	
GDP per capita in Purchasing Power Standards as percentage of EU-15 average in 2000	
Luxembourg	190
Norway	137
Iceland	121
Denmark	120
Ireland	118
Netherlands	117
Belgium	111
Austria	110
Germany	105
UK	104
Finland	103
Italy	102
Sweden	102
France	99
Cyprus	82
Spain	81
Portugal	74
Slovenia	72
Greece	68
Czech Republic	58
Malta	53
Hungary	52
Slovakia	48
Poland	39
Estonia	37
Lithuania	29
Latvia	29
Turkey	29
Romania	27
Bulgaria	24

Source: Eurostat

In East Europe national sovereignty has been one of the prizes gained on the implosion of the Soviet system. But some of the successor states are proving not to work, or at least not to work well. The state apparatus is corrupt and justice maladministered; political party formation is slower than anticipated and disjointed; in many cases, the media is still controlled by the government; municipal government is failing to provide Western-standard public utilities.

An innovatory and autonomous civil society cannot be imposed on peoples that have known nothing other than cynical autocracy. Although the West can and does facilitate the transition to liberalism and capitalism, many people are fearful of Western influences as a source of disintegration and disruption. Representative democracy in Central and Eastern Europe might have to invent itself afresh: if this took the form of an assertion of popular sovereignty, there would be lessons here for the West. Real democratic participation relies on a shared sense of ownership, which may have become significantly loosened within the very large, technocratic and supranational Europe of the European Union.

Enlargement has featured strongly in this discussion of the driving forces behind European integration, as it will in the scenarios themselves. In our view, reuniting East and West Europe is a moral imperative as well as a strategic necessity and an economic opportunity. Meeting in Copenhagen in 1993, the European Council established notionally strict criteria to be met by the applicant states for both economic and democratic convergence. How firmly and for how long will these be respected? It is already clear that some of the twelve accession countries will be ready to join the Union much sooner than others. Then there is the big question of Turkey, a candidate country that is judged not to have yet fulfilled the Copenhagen criteria. The long-term development of the Union is likely to be much influenced by the relative success of existing member states and the first newcomers from Central Europe in coping with the strains and stresses of their new relationship.

The Union's *Agenda 2000* package was designed to cater for enlargement without increasing the ceiling of EU expenditure. One may question whether this constraint is either desirable or realistic, especially as the budget is already under considerable strain as a result of the occupation of Kosovo. If enlargement is to be made to work well to the lasting advantage of all Europe, the financial capacity of the European Union may well need up-grading. More money may be wisely spent in hastening the comprehensive reorientation of the East towards the market economy and democratic civil society. Today, the consumer in Central and Eastern Europe spends about half his or her income on food, compared to roughly 15 per cent within the European Union. That differential will have to close if the trade and investment potential of those countries is to be realised.

There must also be within the candidate countries a revolution in local government, so that they mirror the trend within the existing member states for greater decentralisation. The case for autonomous regional government in a federal Europe is being felt within the larger centralised states of France, Italy, Spain and the UK. Austria, Belgium and Germany are already federal states. Everywhere there is within the European Union a concept of a 'Europe of the Regions' that is not simply about grant-grubbing from Brussels. Scots, Welsh, Basques, Flemish, Lombards, Catalans and Corsicans — and Girondins everywhere — find themselves in the vanguard of those who push for a federal Europe, thereby establishing some important spillover effect of integration.

The future institutional development of the European Union will be affected by how it adapts to the dual challenge of globalisation and localisation. In fact, this tension is one of the fundamental drivers of our scenarios. Its institutions will need to be receptive to broad and highly differentiated participation of a multitude of actors from several territorial levels and functional communities.

The balance between member state governments and the supranational institutions may continue to be unstable, as powers flow back and forth between the two according to economic cycles, political fashion and external or environmental pressures. Alternatively, such a cyclical process may be replaced by a more incremental, steady growth-path towards a new type of federal union.

Federal Union

The key elements of this debate are already well-known: the scope of qualified majority voting and the weighting of votes in the Council; the extension of the European Parliament's budgetary powers and its right to legislative co-decision with the Council; law-making in secret by the Council; the powers, method of appointment and size of the European Commission; the breadth of the jurisdiction of the European Court of Justice; the legitimacy of the European Central Bank; the application of the principle of subsidiarity; and the transfer of competencies from intergovernmental to supranational methods of decision-making, especially in the field of internal and external security.

The Single European Act (1987) followed by the Treaties of Maastricht (1992), Amsterdam (1997) and Nice (2001) have developed European integration but they have not settled the issue of European governance. At Nice, conceding that a new Intergovernmental Conference was needed in 2004, the heads of state and government decided that its agenda shall include *inter alia* the questions of (i) how to "establish and monitor a more precise delimitation of competencies between the European Union and the Member States, reflecting the principle of subsidiarity"; (ii) the status of the Charter of Fundamental Rights; (iii) "a simplification of the Treaties with a view to making them clearer and better understood without changing their meaning"; and (iv) "the role of national parliaments in the European architecture". Accession states will participate in the new conference; candidate states will be invited as observers.

Among the more interesting questions that confront us now is whether the European Union will ever inject itself with elements of more direct federal democracy based on a heightened sense of common European citizenship — such as a directly elected President of the Commission or truly transnational political parties — or whether it will continue to make do with modified versions of the existing institutions and procedures. Above all, will the European Union continue to tolerate a growing pile of relatively obscure and highly complicated Treaties, or will it take the bold step towards a proper constitutional settlement of a federal union?

What we mean by 'federal union' in the contemporary European context is an entity in which state and popular sovereignty is voluntarily pooled. The federal level must have a clearly defined, essential minimum of exclusive competencies. There could also be certain exclusive competencies for member states and, where relevant, regional authorities, although such a multi-tiered catalogue of competency would be inflexible, over-complicated and prone to litigiousness. On balance, we prefer the more pragmatic constitutional approach — setting out what the European Union can do on its own, and leaving everything else to be shared concurrently among the different levels of government. The institutions of this multi-level governance are coordinate with each other, but except in the areas of exclusive competence, not subordinate.

This federative power-sharing accords to two general principles: proportionality and subsidiarity. Proportionality means that government action should be commensurate with the scale of the issue to be addressed. Subsidiarity means that decisions should be taken at the lowest effective level. The whole is run by parliamentary democracy and governed by the rule of law.

Assessing the Outcomes

In the following pages we make a summary of what are, in 2020, the most plausible or likely outcomes of the four main driving forces of demography, technology, globalisation and ideology. Our assessment is categorised under the five broad headings of economics, environment, security, governance and society.

ECONOMICS

Longer, healthier lives have greater economic potential and market opportunities. Health care and recreational spending rises. But growing affluence may blunt entrepreneurship.

Ageing nature of European population means that EU has to deal with 'pensions time bomb' by moving away from pay-as-you-go state schemes to private sector savings which will in turn generate new transnational investment funds. Otherwise, severe taxation burden on workers.

Youth has high incomes to dispose of on accessories.

EU may need to attract immigrant workers. More women in employment, particularly in Southern Europe.

Growing regional disparities.

ENVIRONMENT

A period of tough politics and hard choices, although the more stable population makes environmental management easier.

Increased planning pressures: huge demand on housing as families partition; growing congestion in and sprawl of metropolitan areas.

Danger of desertification in rural areas caused by drought, depopulation and global warming.

Problems of food, water and infrastructure.

SECURITY

Low European fertility plus high fertility in near-abroad, especially Maghreb, causes increased pressure for immigration.

Challenge to social cohesion.

Larger immigrant population imports its own feuds.

Retired white-collar workers migrate southwards within EU.

EU integrates its border patrols.

GOVERNANCE

Government provides a variety of social services to those who choose to contribute and buy them. EU buttresses national systems, but only if accompanied by decentralisation.

New generation of active elderly are a strong and mainly conservative political lobby.

Trend of fiscal policy throughout EU shifts welfare spending from public to private sector.

Greater social dislocation and regional divergence makes governance more complex still.

Common asylum and immigration policy.

High profile overseas aid and development policy, although spending clashes with needs of the ageing domestic population.

SOCIETY

Social insurance no longer a key element of social democracy.

Changing profile of working lifetime. Younger generation under pressure to perform academically and economically. Social tensions within families and communities between young and old leads to volatile labour market, greater mobility and self-assertive youth.

Divorce rate grows in Southern Europe towards Northern norm.

Elderly work (and retrain) longer. Child care at a premium.

Development of mutual schemes.

Challenge of multi-ethnicity, as immigration flows hit high levels.

DRIVING FORCE: TECHNOLOGY 2020

ECONOMICS

Productivity gains from networked Europe.

Economies of scale become less important.

Traditional postal services and retailing close. Integration of the computer and telecoms businesses.

Rapid hardware obsolescence. Continued fall in price-to-power ratio.

New systems of production and infrastructure, with convergence of financial services, retailing, media and utilities.

Taxation attempted on the international flow of megabytes.

Monopolistic behaviour of high-tech companies impedes growth and technology transfer.

Conservation and re-cycling are growth sectors.

Greater regional disparity.

ENVIRONMENT

Innovation helps clean up industry and agriculture, and transforms health care — although biotechnology advances create new risks and challenges for both governments and environmentalists.

Designer drugs tailored to individual patients.

Growth of service sector reduces EU emissions of greenhouse gas.

European conservation know-how flourishes world-wide.

EU faces critical choice between nuclear and renewable energy sources.

Possible major catastrophe.

SECURITY

EU pioneers UN reform.

Generally increasing Western advantage, but asymmetric defence predicament as technology changes nature of conflict. EU and Nato face non-traditional military threats.

Very high cost of non-Europe in defence industries poses questions about transatlantic relationship, but also speeds integration of European industry.

Growing reliance on early conflict prevention rather than late military intervention.

Controversy over ownership and policing of intellectual property rights.

High risk of intrusive surveillance. Computer crime perennial: EU represented by Europol, the European FBI.

GOVERNANCE

Controversial integrated European defence industry serves to build common foreign and security policy.

EU institutions try to galvanise mass participation in electronic referenda: endless consultation.

Political institutions more responsive to market research — although less responsible about data protection.

Rise of anti-progress parties.

Governments pay high premium for best scientific advice.

New education emphasis on distance learning and technology training for the elderly.

EU-US relations under strain, especially over divergent attitudes to security and defence spending.

SOCIETY

Cash rich, time poor society. Within the EU, 85 per cent of homes use the internet for work and play on a daily basis.

Big divide between the majority who are IT users and the rest. Virtual communities replace real communities for IT-obsessed youth.

Technophobia also emerges. E-mail overload provokes nostalgia for more 'natural' lifestyles.

Power of global multi-media, widespread use of smart cards and genetic modification raises fears about liberty, privacy and ethics.

Spread of IT permits more consultative approach by companies and more participative approach by a dispersed workforce.

Societal trend is towards team effort, flexibility and decentralisation.

ECONOMICS

Rapid growth of transnational portfolio investment. Balance of power shifts from individual state actors to multinational mega-corporations.

Euro and dollar dominate global finance, but huge global money flows prompt efforts at international regulation and benchmarking. Taxation mooted on international capital movements, possibly hypothecated by World Bank to aid least developed countries.

Restructuring of European companies, especially in IT, arms, transport and finance. Hiving off of non-core activities to smaller enterprises.

Liberation of market innovators favours new products and emerging markets.

Europe shrinks its production of goods and shifts further to services.

Big effort to increase trade and investment in Central and Eastern Europe.

High cost to business of environmental audits.

ENVIRONMENT

Environmental standards differ widely between EU and rest of world. EU is forced to pay the developing world to bridge the gap between investment in low cost, high polluting projects on the one hand and sustainable development on the other.

Environmental audits more rigorous.

Global segmentation of production along environmental lines.

Much depends on balance of food supply and consumption world-wide. European agriculture has to adapt.

Rise of environmental crime.

Pressure builds within WTO for more eco-taxation as concern about global warming increases.

Possible major catastrophe.

SECURITY

EU and Nato challenged to play a world-wide role, possibly in desperation. Tensions between EU and US.

China overtakes Russia as potential destabiliser of world order; but Russia remains awkward near-neighbour.

More competition world-wide for scarce resources.

EU member states individually may or may not tackle structural unemployment, with different social consequences.

Terrorists target key companies in energy, financial and high technology sectors.

Global coalitions of disgruntled launch mass civil disobedience via the internet.

Arms trade more volatile. International crime flourishes, especially drugs trafficking.

More mobility raises mutual understanding but undermines security and induces more regulation everywhere.

GOVERNANCE

EU leads transformation of WTO to become world regulatory and competition authority. G3 (USA, Emergent Asia, EU) tries to hold the ring.

High level of Western investment in Asia, but tension persists between human rights and liberal democracy of the West and more authoritarian Eastern models of government.

Within EU, Ecofin becomes cabinet for macro-economic policy-making. Member states lose control and, over time, shed pretensions.

Decline or adaptation of traditional political parties; rise of post-national NGOs. Rise of trans-European political class.

EU citizenship under strain from legitimate expectations of non-nationals.

Ineffective regulation resisted. But environmental audits put more pressure on public administration.

SOCIETY

Attempt to preserve European social values in teeth of global competition. But public begin to prefer international benchmarking on taxation and standards of service.

Public welfare systems decline vis-à-vis comprehensive private sector protection.

Pressurised working conditions in more open and competitive markets undermine family and social life — yet demand for more education and training. Growth in voluntary sector or 'para' work, self-employment and mobility.

Spread of American-English. But multi-culturalism makes slow advance. Contrasting role for women in Christian and Islamic communities.

Growth of networked NGOs and extra-parliamentary activism, especially in ethical and environmental matters.

DRIVING FORCE: IDEOLOGY 2020

ECONOMICS

Rise of new ideology of global market interventionism as escape route from economic amorality and laissez-faire.

The value of probity and practice of financial supervision increasingly adopted world-wide.

Triumph of neo-liberalism in post-national EU provokes reaction, especially in peripheral regions.

Successful experiments at local level at cooperation in mutual societies. Role of market forces reassessed.

Partnerships between business and NGOs.

Taxation of functional communities which, to avoid cartelisation, embrace both producers and consumers.

ENVIRONMENT

Battle of subsidiarity about where best to exercise authority in environmental matters.

Europeans try to project the values of sustainable development world-wide.

Broad support for eco-taxes within EU.

Mainstream environmentalism embedded, but reaction sets in against puritanical greenery.

SECURITY

The UN, trying to cope with enhanced security responsibilities, spawns debate about world government.

'European Citizenship' provokes neo-liberal and nationalist reaction. Failure to build a new European identity may leave a vacuum. Identities and loyalties contested. Immature European demos.

Reaction against too much government.

Within EU, enhanced legal regime required to allow toleration of and arbitration between strongly conflicting interests. EU Bill of Rights.

EU joins USA as possible target for protests against its increasing projection of political and military power.

GOVERNANCE

Difficult multi-level governance judgements about resource allocation and social cohesion.

Europe leads quest for world-wide legal and political norms that permit stable and sustainable development and take advantage of IT revolution and globalisation.

Europeans try to project the values of good governance and independent judiciary world-wide: benign imperialism.

Europe is over-governed. General disenchantment with government. Europeans question the continuing role of the traditional regime of the state. 'New federalism' emerges, with emphasis on decentralisation and individual autonomy.

Decline of concept of nation-state sovereignty; rise of popular sovereignty. Demand for more direct democracy. Possible rise of functional rather than geographic communities.

SOCIETY

Tension between traditional European social contract and imperative of privatisation and deregulation.

Most EU citizens focus on their own terms and conditions of work. New federalism also informs restructuring of companies.

Competitive spirit complements raised awareness of the role of women and children.

Enhanced civil society role for NGOs pitches values of neo-corporatism against those of individual citizenship.

Mutual tolerance under stress.

The value of combating poverty increasingly accepted world-wide.

Religions forced to compete with each other directly: first multi-faith negotiations between Christians, Moslems and Jews.

PART TWO

Alternative Scenarios of the Future of Europe

Having examined the main driving forces that are likely to shape Europe's future, and having made an assessment of their possible outcomes, it is fairly clear that Europe can ill afford to leave much to destiny. For the leadership of the European Union, in particular, political choices matter. Good opportunities missed, like the Treaty of Nice, might not return. Time presses. Alternative scenarios might help to concentrate the mind.

Models for scenarios

The Federal Trust undertook an earlier scenarios exercise in 1990.[6] At that stage, the European Community had only twelve member states, the single market programme was far from completion and the Maastricht Treaty had yet to be negotiated. The internet had hardly impinged on us, and mobile phones were large, clumsy, erratic and expensive. The Balkans, although troubled, were still relatively peaceful. The Soviet Union and Czechoslovakia were still extant. Margaret Thatcher was British prime minister.

The Trust offered four alternative scenarios in the perspective of 2010, as follows:

> 1. **A Multi-Tier Europe**, in which 'the core countries of the European Community continue to strengthen their links across a widening range of economic and social issues, whilst other European countries develop such links to a more limited degree and at a slower pace.'

58

2. **A Wide and Strong European Community**, which would be 'an enlarged Community with strengthened powers comprising economic and monetary union, tougher environmental protection and a common foreign and security policy, and with institutions reformed so as to make majority voting the general rule in the Council and to give the European Parliament the right of co-decision with it.'

3. **A Wide but Weak European Community**, where the Community 'would remain roughly at its present [1991] level of integration: deeply integrated in certain respects such as agriculture, external trade and the single market, but with only shallow integration in other areas such as monetary, fiscal and foreign policy. The principle of subsidiarity would be invoked to limit the power of the Community institutions and to retain as much competence as possible with the member states.'

4. **A Disintegrating Europe**, 'with a supranational German-led core and several 'off-shore' arrangements managed (rather badly) by intergovernmental diplomacy. These peripheral groups could centre on the Mediterranean, Russia, Scandinavia and Britain. This would be a Europe plagued by instability and struggling with disunity in an increasingly mercantilist world.'

As the Millennium approached, there was an anticipated flurry of forecasting and scenario-building from a number of reputable sources. We describe the most notable here.

In 1996 the Royal Institute of International Affairs in London published three scenarios concerning the whole of the industrialised world, Europe included, in the perspective of 2015.[7] They were:

1. **Faster, Faster**, where 'the competent nations of 2015 know what they have to do in order to survive. Every nation is doing it, therefore, to the best of its abilities. Sources of advantage are becoming increasingly scant. Specialisation is everywhere evident, but this somehow fails to convey much advantage ..... Those who will not run, or who stumble, suffer huge penalties.'

2. **The Post-Industrial Revolution**, in which the societies of the industrialised world 'have proved to be potent in their ability to generate knowledge and to pick up and use this knowledge ..... [P]eople feel a restored sense of competence: of operating in a local environment which they understand and trust, of having something with which they can

identify as a community and source of identity and, above all, of being in a position to take charge of their own fate.'

3. **Rough Neighbours**, where 'the conditions of **Faster, Faster** develop with intolerable speed. More and more of the industrialised world countries find the demands of change to be socially unmanageable ..... Social reaction against commercial and state adjustment processes leads, in a vicious spiral, to worsening commercial performance and to intensifying social impact.'

For Michael Emerson (1998), European nationalism has already had its day. He identifies three paradigms as relevant in shaping the emerging map of Europe: federalism, a looser 'cosmopolitan democracy' and the application of corporate management techniques.[8] European integration, he suggests, will not achieve the territorial stability of the USA, and, in any case, will never be the assimilating melting pot that has fashioned the American federal experience. The many over-lapping international organisations in the European region within the globalised economy will instead engender a post-modern style of cosmopolitan democracy in which corporate management techniques, aided by information technology, will be the order of the day. Emerson offers four alternative maps, finding the last the most desirable but also the most elusive:

1. **Europe of two blocks**, of the EU and Russia.

2. **Brussels Europe**, an introverted EU, with Russia, Ukraine and Turkey left to pursue their own destinies.

3. **Security Europe**, all OSCE countries, with a Nato core and a continuing, but ambiguous US presence.

4. **Civil Europe**, based on the Council of Europe, with a strong EU core and pan-European economic collaboration.

Andersen Consulting have recently devised three scenarios for their corporate customers.[9] According to them, Europe in 2008 will be one of the following:

1. **Competitive Europe**, 'a shareholder model of capitalism within an integrated and enlarged Europe with a Single Market and single currency. Powerful central institutions promote competition, having abolished subsidies and removed trade barriers. The labour market is very lightly regulated, and the gap between rich and poor is widening. Mergers, acquisitions and new entrants transform the corporate landscape.'

2. **Conscience Europe**, which is a 'stakeholder' model of capitalism, where the EU directs 'both economic and social policies, with the aim of ensuring high minimum social and environmental standards, and protecting vital industries against foreign competition. Companies treat staff as long-term assets, although high social costs also mean there is an emphasis on capital-intensive investment.'

3. **Patchwork Europe**, 'a fragmented Europe, where power has become devolved to national and sub-national bodies. Different 'regions' have emerged, from city-states through to loose cross-border groupings, each pursuing different socio-economic models. Europe comprises a patchwork of very different environments for business, with some regions espousing undiluted free-market capitalism, while others apply a new kind of communitarian socialism and a third group practice more traditional forms of interventionism. Trade barriers have reappeared, as have different currencies.'

The question of big state small state relations, and in particular the future of Germany, features in a contribution from the Netherlands Institute of International Relations at Clingendael. The Dutch team also draw out the contrast between economic and military factors, also with a horizon of 2020. Their five scenarios are:

1. **Europe in Tutelage**, The integration of the EU continues, but in security matters Europe remains subordinate to the USA. This scenario 'represents in important respects a continuation of the status quo.'

2. **Muscular Europe**, The EU develops into an independent political and military entity under Franco-German-British leadership, 'a development that will lead to alienation between Europe and the US.'

3. **Europe in a Shambles**, The EU disintegrates and falls victim to the 'old reflexes of power rivalry, nationalism and shifting coalitions. German-Russian antagonism will dominate the European scene.'

4. **Mercantilist Europe**, Europe is a trade bloc that shields itself from the outside world to protect its social and ecological standards.

5. **Globalised Europe**, 'As a consequence of rapid and large-scale expansion, Europe will dilute into a pan-European, free trade zone. However, this zone of market-oriented democracies will constitute an integral part of a largely economised, multilateral and peaceful world system.'[10]

The accountants PricewaterhouseCoopers offered us four scenarios for 'New Europe' in 2010.[11]

1. **The Golden Triangle**, 'steady growth, open markets and technological advance.'

2. **On the Edge**, 'strong but highly unstable growth driven by break-neck technological progress and fierce competition.'

3. **The Last Castle**, 'governments slam on the regulatory and protectionist brakes as public opinion revolts against rising economic insecurity.'

4. **Drowning Spires**, 'accelerating climate change, social unrest, economic disruption and green politics in the ascendant.'

Rosemary Radcliffe, the firm's Chief Economist, concluded in the light of these scenarios that businesses should adopt a four-fold strategy involving:

• global reach and geographical diversification of economic risk;

• operational flexibility — 'small is beautiful' even in the largest companies;

• local presence — to avoid trade barriers and guarantee a voice in public policy debates;

• heightened environmental awareness and investment.

Finally, we have also followed with interest the work of the Forward Studies Unit of the European Commission which, after a 'structured brainstorming' lasting two years, has published five stimulating futures for Europe in 2010.[12]

1. **Triumphant Markets**, Europe adjusts to globalisation at the cost of reducing social and environmental standards. The political project of building Europe is abandoned, but economic growth soars.

2. **The Hundred Flowers**, A reaction against strong government, consumerism and corporatism leads to a greater emphasis on local communities. The fragmentation of the economy means wide variations between regions, with a large black economy. European integration stagnates.

3. **Shared Responsibilities**, Structural reform of the welfare state systems encourages responsible citizenship, public private partnerships and a dynamic, redistributive budget. A clear consensus about the

finalité politique of the EU emerges; Europe becomes the defender of civilisation abroad.

4. **Creative Societies**, A social and economic crisis brought about by the pressures of Economic and Monetary Union has led to a new start for the single currency, marked by stronger cohesion and lower growth. Integration proceeds in justice and home affairs, but not much else. EU incoherence in relation to the East and South.

5. **Turbulent Neighbourhoods**, The EU is embroiled in military conflicts, many of them provoked by water shortage. Economic and social reforms are halted almost everywhere. The US has withdrawn from Europe, and the weakened EU institutions struggle to cope. Globalisation is causing monetary instability and a growing divergence of wealth and health between rich and poor.

The Commission's study postulates an ambitious reform in a federal direction of an enlarged EU only in 'Shared Responsibilities.' Here, the Council has been split into three *collegia* of large, medium and small member states; there has been large-scale decentralisation of EU administration, and involvement of civil society. 'The Hundred Flowers' scenario sees greater differentiation between member states within the Union. Prospects for Central and Eastern Europe are also best in these two scenarios: otherwise, economic and political development in these regions is patchy. America dominates 'Triumphant Markets'; Russia fares well in this buccaneering environment, but also in 'Shared Responsibilities.'

Developing scenarios

In contrasting scenarios, one is faced inevitably with methodological difficulty in measuring progress or change and in making comparisons in the economic, social, cultural and environmental development of states and their peoples. We are also aware that, first, no matter how sophisticated the scenario, unpredictable and catastrophic events are likely to occur and that, second, there are sciences yet to be discovered and new fashions to burgeon.

From the scenarios summarised above, despite their rich variety of approach, certain common themes emerge in their stories about the future of Europe which could be translated into the arena of political choice:

➢ the concept of what Chatham House calls the 'competent nation,' and strengths and weaknesses of the representative capability of political authority;

➢ a perceived tension between competitive market forces and the pull of social conscience — Andersen Consulting's 'shareholder' and 'stakeholder' capitalism, respectively;

➢ protectionist blocs versus open frontiers;

➢ steady growth or volatility;

➢ centralisation of authority as opposed to fragmentation;

➢ a civilian or a military Europe.

Our own focus, again slightly different, is to show how the driving forces might affect the constitutional development of the European Union. We do not start from the presumption that the EU is already a uniform political entity. Although fifty years of European integration has brought the stance and attitudes of different countries closer together, there are still marked divergences between member states about where the Union is and should be headed. Some are more inclined to rely on the power of market forces than of state authority; others prefer the concept of the traditional nation state to that of federation. Along these two axes, it is possible to plot the contrasting current positions and tendencies of, for example, Britain, France, Germany and Italy as shown in the chart below:

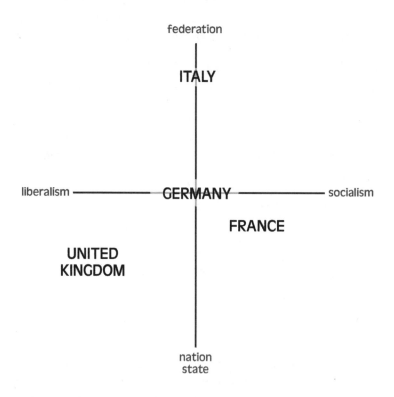

If existing trends continue, we would expect these different national views to converge over time. We would *hope* that all Europe shifts deliberately inside the triangle, as shown below, and that the rest of the world is encouraged to follow suit. Our golden triangle, in contrast to PricewaterhouseCoopers's, is formed by three processes: integration, efficiency and democracy.

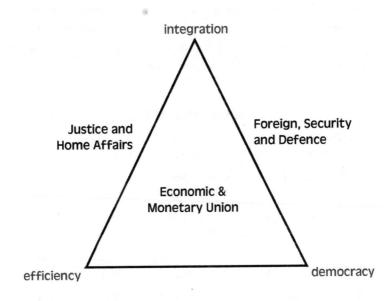

Again, as examples, whereas monetary policy is already featured centrally, common foreign and security policy is as yet neither very integrated nor efficient, while internal security policy is increasingly integrated and efficient but not very democratic. To attract all policy sectors towards the triangle and to manage their interdependence within the context of federal union seems to us to be a feasible objective. In historical terms, such an outcome would be for Europe and the world benign, although still not without risk.

Taken in a long perspective, are we right to assume an onward march of liberal democracy? On the basis of the past evidence of modern European history since the end of the American and French Revolutions, probably. During this period, and notwithstanding wars, plagues, famines, earthquakes, floods and revolutions, the number of states with a justifiable claim to call themselves free democracies continued to grow. As the table below reminds us, the march of democracy has been closely associated with market liberalisation and improvements to communications.

EUROPE 1800-2000

1820 - Post-Enlightenment, balance of power Europe; partial liberalisation; growth of trade; telegraph technology.

1870 - European imperialism and state-building; industrial development; globalisation; telephone technology.

1920 - Rise of fascism and communism; centralised economies; protectionism; radio and television.

1970 - Post-Holocaust Europe; partial liberalisation; early integration; transistor, computer, satellite and optical fibre technology.

2000 - Post-national Europe; return to globalisation; mature integration; internet and human genome.

Democracy and the market are powerful paradigms, eclipsing all others on the world stage. But they are also ambiguous concepts, whose meaning has changed and continues to change, not least as the traditional confines of the nation state become less cosy and even irrelevant. And, as we have discussed in the first part of this book, the very familiarity of our paradigms may breed contempt, or at least a misplaced complacency about their entrenchment and permanence. That is why we would stress the importance of continual reform, the imperative of which seems to us to be just as important in the old market democracies of Western Europe and North America as it is in the new democracies of Eastern Europe and Latin America, or in the emerging democracies of Africa and Asia.

Based on this analysis and derived from our driving forces and their plausible outcomes, we first offer three alternative scenarios for Europe's futures.

The three are:

1. Superstate Europa

2. Flexible Europe

3. Europe Adrift

None of these scenarios constitute our ideal choice. We would draw on the lessons of each scenario to enable us to be prescriptive about what should, as opposed to might, happen.

Finally, therefore, we publish as an example of what might develop out of any of the three scenarios, a possible constitution for a federal union of Europe. This is by way of being our fourth alternative scenario, and takes the form of a preamble and thirteen constituent articles, most of which are inspired by the existing Treaties, with which, indeed, they are intended to be consistent. The institutional set-up will be familiar to any student of the current European Union, while not being identical with it.

Such a federal union could be broad in its membership (there is also provision for associate membership) as well as deep in its effect. People would know, more or less — and certainly more so than now — how they are governed, by whom and from where. The political system would be less unsettled. Who does what will be less controversial than the quality of public policy that comes from Europe. To be 'pro-European' or 'anti-European' would be barely relevant, just as in today's United Kingdom one's sympathy or antipathy for Westminster is seldom a defining feature of political opinion. In twenty years time, in other words, the future of Europe as a whole could be more democratic, less threatening for the states, and more engaging for the citizen.

SCENARIO 1: *SUPERSTATE EUROPA*

Eighteen states belong to the United States of Europe (USE): the current fifteen members of the European Union plus Iceland, Norway and Switzerland. No further enlargement has yet proved possible.

Protracted EU accession negotiations with several other states stumbled as the existing member states, aided and abetted by the Commission and Parliament, persistently raised the threshold for membership. The Charter of Fundamental Rights and the Treaty of Nice was followed by an ambitious reform of the Treaties in 2004 which strengthened the federal powers of the Union, especially in economic policy. Entry to the euro became consequently more difficult, as did the demands made on member states in the field of external border control, police and judicial cooperation. Faced with the higher price of entry, public opinion in the candidate countries turned sullenly against membership.

The enlargement project collapsed completely in the aftermath of the Crimean War (2010-11), in which the USA and the European Union, while remaining non-belligerents, backed different sides. Nato collapsed after right-wing US Republican President Su Chang, supported by Congress, effectively stopped the Europeans from intervening to support Greece when Turkey took advantage of the war in the Crimea to re-invade Cyprus. The US withheld intelligence and logistical assistance from the EU. (Some suspected the CIA of engineering the whole thing.)

In 2013, in the aftermath of the crisis, the Europeans adopted by referendum a new constitution, negotiated by the governments at a congress in Berlin, that turned the European Union plus the vestiges of the Western European Union into the 'United States of Europe.'

Collective defence became an exclusive competence of the federal government. The new Combined European Defence Force (CEDF) is now fully operational in border patrol duties, peace-keeping in the Balkans and the Caucasus, and on special missions in Africa (at the moment, Sudan, Eritrea and the Congo), the Middle East and Kashmir. Its units police Cyprus and Palestine, as well as Georgia and the Western half of the Ukraine, based in

Lvov. Albania, Bosnia-Herzegovina, Croatia, Kosovo, Montenegro, Serbia and Macedonia form provinces of the USE's Balkan Dominion. Negotiations for the sale of Kaliningrad to the USE continue.

The CEDF has incorporated the former national armed forces of all the member states, including the nuclear forces of Britain and France, and is responsible for all arms procurement. It is a fully professional force, although it is now building up a large reserve force conscripted from those who fail to pass the Euro-baccalaureate. To date, HQ in Brussels has managed to lease from the Russians heavy-lift transport planes, but the restructured European armaments industry, which is enjoying something of a boom, is on stream to provide an independent transport capacity within the next year or two, and new satellite weapons systems. Hawks are campaigning for the launch of a USE space station.

After it succeeded in partitioning the Ukraine and Moldova, an exhausted Russia collapsed into warring provinces. Embattled especially on its eastern and southern frontiers, Moscow was unable to maintain the loyalty of its provinces beyond the Urals. Contingency preparations to limit the impact of chaos in Russia feature prominently in the strategic planning of the CEDF. Turkey, rejected by Europe, pursues Islamist options, and has formed an alliance with Afghanistan, Tajikistan, Turkmenistan and Azerbaijan. Israel, now allied to a revisionist Iran as well as the USA, is threatened by more concerted Arab pressure.

Despite the tense nature of the transatlantic relationship, a new Atlantic Treaty was signed by the USE, USA and Canada in 2018 re-committing both sides to security cooperation worldwide. However, the American troop withdrawal from USE territory will not be reversed. Relations have worsened recently after the 'Hot Box Scandal,' when an American spy ring was exposed at work in Cambridge, England. And US moves to recruit its base of Malta as the 52nd American state have not exactly eased Euro-American relations.

China, admitted to the WTO, and now enjoying the highest GDP in the world, plays off American and European interests. South Asia is another arena for proxy Euro-American rivalry.

The USE has assumed the permanent seats of France and the United Kingdom in the UN Security Council — although the UN remains unreformed, divided and ineffectual. None of the Permanent Members has been willing to support reform initiatives led by South Africa and Australia. The USE also has single representation in the IMF, the World Bank and the OSCE.

Tony Blair took office in January 2015, at the age of 61, as President of the United States of Europe, having been elected by direct universal suffrage. His five year term has been dominated by international relations, and especially by his efforts to resolve the Crimean War and to effect Turkish withdrawal from Cyprus. He has succeeded in scheduling talks to explore the possibility of a Pan-European Security Treaty, based on the old, but redundant, OSCE.

The euro is the major world currency. An exchange rate mechanism linking the euro and the dollar was set up in 2008 but collapsed four years later under the weight of its own contradictions. With defence spending a major item, Ecofin has become responsible for a USE budget amounting to some 7 per cent of GDP or $ 600 billion (compared to $ 90 billion in 2000). The government's efforts to centralise fiscal policy were at first strongly resisted by a minority of member states, notably Britain and Denmark, but the Court of Justice has upheld the centralising policy of the Commission and Council, invoking the constitutional principle of subsidiarity.

Public opinion has been fairly supportive of the shift of expenditure from the national to the European basis. Opinion polls show that common defence and transport spending are consistently the most popular items of the USE budget, even in those regions, notably the Mezzogiorno, that experienced a period of intensified unemployment and social unrest. Likewise, the European Central Bank is shown to be the most trusted of all the USE institutions, despite (or because of) the attacks it has suffered from both the extreme left and the right. Economic growth has been fairly steady at an annual average of 2.5 per cent; inflation is negligible; interest rates stable; unemployment variable.

Trans-European Networks have revolutionised transport within all member states and beyond them. A comprehensive programme of integrated autoroute and high-speed rail networks is about two-thirds completed, stretching, as it were, from Galway to St Petersburg and from Oslo to Athens. The route from Budapest to Istanbul is scheduled for completion in five years time. After the air traffic control disasters of the 2000s, the federal aviation authority (EFAA) has also proved its worth.

Italy and Spain, like the UK, have themselves become fully federal states. After considerable political turbulence, France has reached a new concordat which many suppose is only a transitional arrangement before the federalisation process is completed there too. All autonomous regional parliaments have participatory rights in USE decision-making as well as the right of recourse in the European Court of Justice.

Within the USE the privilege of freedom of movement of persons applies only to USE citizens. Under the common asylum and immigration policy each state of the Union has to accept an ordained quota of new-comers, although these quotas are now traded between states. The Commission was rebuffed by the Court in its attempt to stop this practice. Official immigration is now running at 350,000 a year, many of whom are skilled workers from Asia.

USE sheriffs or *intendants*, appointed directly by Brussels and backed up by Europol, oversee the implementation of common policy in agricultural, industrial, trade, employment, immigration, environmental, planning, food hygiene, animal welfare and transport affairs. Only health, housing and most aspects of educational and social security policy remain national responsibilities. Competition and state aids policy is run by the powerful federal anti-cartel agency (EFACA).

President Blair chairs both the Commission, his executive, and also the Council, which is now composed of senior cabinet ministers for European affairs who are effectively deputy prime ministers of their respective states. The President is also Commander-in-Chief of the CEDF.

The Council uses qualified majority voting (over half the states representing over half the population) across the board, although decisions to go to war, to admit a new member state, or to change the constitution have to achieve a 'super QMV' of two-thirds of states. In addition, revision of the constitution requires a popular referendum.

The President also presides over the regular bi-annual (and occasional crisis) meetings of the European Council of heads of government. Only the annual ceremonial meetings of the heads of state retain the six-monthly presidency of each member state, a role which King William V seems ready to relish.

Besides the President, who is directly elected on the same day as the European Parliament, the Commission has twelve other members, of whom four are Vice-Presidents responsible for the large portfolios of the economy, the environment, the budget, foreign affairs and defence. Each member state is guaranteed to have its nomination selected as a member of the Commission at least every second mandate (that is, once every ten years). Mr Blair's successor has caused a stir by electing not to choose the British government's nominee to join the Commission that will take office in January 2020, but she seems to have the support of her former colleagues in the European Parliament in that decision.

All USE laws have to be passed both by the Council and the European Parliament. The Parliament is also a participant in the process of amending the constitution. European Parliamentary elections are held according to a uniform electoral procedure, and attract a turnout of about 60 per cent. 70 MEPs, a tenth of the total, are elected from a supranational list. There are single European political parties, to the big four of which (Progressive Conservatives, Socialists, Liberals and Greens) 90 per cent of MEPs belong.

The Charter of Fundamental Rights is mandatory upon all USE institutions, member state and regional governments. Citizens have become privileged litigants at the Court of Justice, which has assumed the role of a federal supreme court with consummate ease.

The Parliament has become very powerful and is the centre of heavy media and lobby attention. It has upset a number of national governments by seeking to intervene in decisions about how USE law and policy is implemented on the ground. Its committees of inquiry have exposed much malpractice in the use of USE funds, particularly under the old CAP. It has also not been backward in using its new powers over USE revenue to promote common taxation.

Worries about creeping over-centralisation of the United States of Europe, not least over fiscal policy, have spawned a powerful constitutional reform movement. A Convention is completing a new draft of the federal constitution which will more clearly and simply delimit the powers of the union. This has already received the backing of the European Parliament, and it is now up to the member state governments to decide to put it to a referendum in 2021.

The change involves a reversion to the original title of 'European Union,' as well as the ability of a member state to negotiate its secession. The President of the Commission will no longer be directly elected, but appointed jointly by the European Council and Parliament.

The new constitution is expected to pass into law. It is hoped that the reform will induce a new phase of more constructive European engagement with the USA as well as serve to open up once again the question of an enlarged membership for the Union. There is growing pressure from the former candidate countries, led by Poland, for the reopening of membership negotiations. Although they have enjoyed increasing trade with the USE and have derived considerable benefits from USE investment in joint environmental, R&D and transport programmes, their strategic position has remained insecure. This time enlargement must be for real.

SCENARIO 2: *FLEXIBLE EUROPE*

By 2020 membership of the European Union has grown to thirty-seven states, comprising the eighteen member states of *Superstate Europa* plus Albania, Bosnia-Herzegovina, Bulgaria, Croatia, Cyprus, the Czech Republic, Estonia, Hungary, Kosovo, Latvia, Lithuania, Macedonia, Malta, Poland, Romania, Serbia-Montenegro, Slovakia, Slovenia and Turkey. Armenia, Georgia, Moldova and the Ukraine are candidate countries. The Union is also considering the status of Algeria, Tunisia and Morocco, which have recently applied to join.

Since the Treaty of Nice came into force in 2002, there has been much greater differentiation — or 'flexibility' — between member states. The Union is now organised into three concentric circles. A solid core of seven West European states enjoy close federal relations over a wide spectrum of policy. A second group either subscribe to the same objectives as the core group but have not yet reached a state of development sufficient for them to join, or do not subscribe to the same objectives and have no wish to join. A third, outer tier, mostly from the Balkans, has negotiated a reduced form of membership of the Union and enjoy a bare minimum of mutual commitment and influence. The United Kingdom briefly joined the third group after the Conservative government was formed following the general election of 2009, but the ensuing domestic crisis resulted in a pro-European coalition government of all the talents which re-negotiated Britain's way back into the second tier.

The variegated form of membership was set in train at the European Council of Nice when the unilateral right of any member state to block the development of differentiated forms of integration, prescribed by the Treaty of Amsterdam, was removed. Germany and France immediately led the first 'pioneer group' of states to reinforce the economic policy of the euro-zone. A special Council of the then twelve euro-zone members was set up despite a challenge by the UK in the Court of Justice. The vanguard went much further ahead in reinforcing their cooperation when the Italian government defaulted on its commitments under the Stability Pact. A new budget, drawn up by the euro-zone Council of Finance Ministers, was e-mailed to Rome.

A common system of corporation tax was introduced by the euro members to reduce competition between member states, and part of the revenue from the common company tax was accorded to a new common eurozone budget designed to be used in a contra-cyclical way to soften the destabilising impact of out-of-kilter national economies.

The sharper differentiation of the euro group of member states created a precedent which was then followed by the Scandinavians (including Estonia), Benelux and Germany to go faster and further in the direction of a single environmental policy. An eco-tax was introduced by those nine member states. This time the legal challenge by the UK, supported by France, was successful. The Court of Justice ordered the dismantling of the special green group on the grounds that such closer cooperation would jeopardise the integrity of the single market. Popular reaction against the enforcement of this judgment, especially in Denmark and Norway, was intense. The Scandinavian and Baltic states then established a new regional union for ecology, based on the precedent of Benelux and in conformity with the Treaty.

Flexibility was deployed without inhibition in the second and third pillars of the Union catering for foreign and security policy and interior affairs. It proved difficult to reconcile the interests of the non-Nato members of the European Union with the non-European members of Nato. Washington proves a more and more reluctant ally. A single EU army corps — 'rapid reaction force' — of 60,000 troops was established by 2005, but Ireland, Scandinavia and the Baltic States effectively vetoed its deployment for anything other than humanitarian missions. This meant that the Union had to stand aside from the Third Balkan War when the Serbs, fresh from their success in suppressing the revolt in Montenegro, tried to re-take Kosovo. (Belgrade was eventually stopped only after the large-scale intervention of the Americans and Turks.) An unhappy compromise was later reached whereby troops under British, French and, more recently, Turkish command work as mercenaries both inside and outside the former Nato theatre, paid for by a combination of other states but not necessarily by the EU itself. This has led to serious political and operational difficulties, not least in the Middle East where cohesion between the UK, France and Turkey is difficult to sustain. 'Common foreign and security policy' is something of a fiction.

In the absence of any credible external security policy, progress towards real freedom of movement of people is halted. Even the euro-zone group has not succeeded in abolishing internal frontiers. Britain and Ireland maintain their special measures, and strict border controls were reintroduced by France, Germany, Austria and Switzerland in an attempt to stop the influx of illegal immigrants to northern Europe. Despite fierce objections from Spain, Italy and Greece, the Benelux have now joined with the core four countries to create a new 'regional justice union.' This 'Innsbruck Pact' was negotiated secretly and, to overcome the objections of their partners, is outside the Treaty on European Union and does not use the common institutions. The Executive Committee of the Innsbruck Seven is developing a veritable fortress policy at the centre of the Union that is clearly intended to achieve a unique and advanced form of political integration that will in the end be indistinguishable from a federal state. The UK is an awkward by-stander in this process, committed to the single currency and to its defence arrangements with France, but unwilling to join the Seven for other reasons. Of the older member states, Finland, Spain, Portugal, Ireland, Italy and Greece would be willing to join but are not invited to do so. Sweden alone is suited.

The Charter of Fundamental Rights is considered binding only by certain member states: to date, the Innsbrück Seven plus Italy and Portugal. Such differentiation presents the Court of Justice with a very real problem in seeking to ensure legal certainty in respect of human rights. The Charter's claim to assert the indivisibility and universality of rights is wearing thin under the weight of competing case law. Its variable interpretation is causing strain not only between EU member states but also within them: the Scottish government, for example, tends to call the Charter in aid in its litigation against the United Kingdom.

In reaction to the Innsbruck agreement, Poland and Hungary have taken the lead in formalising coordination between the Central European member states.

Such all pervasive flexibility has created a fractious atmosphere which in turn has badly weakened the solidarity of the Union. The Commission, with one nominee from each member state, is a pale shadow of its former self at its apogee in the days of Jacques Delors, and is reduced more and more to playing a merely regulatory role — although the centrality of transnational regulation to maintaining the Union should not be underestimated. The regulatory scope of the Commission now includes the media, food hygiene, animal welfare, pollution and financial services as well as industrial competition and state aids policy.

The EU budget amounts to only 2 per cent of GDP, and spending is concentrated on regional development funds, overseas aid and R&D, education and training. Internal and external security activities are paid for separately by national quotas. Agriculture is co-financed on a 50-50 basis by the EU and its member states.

The Presidency of the Council rotates between regional groupings of member states. Unanimity is still the order of the day in all but single market matters. Even the emergency aid package to Bulgaria, Greece and Turkey for the great fire that raged throughout the Aegean during the whole summer of 2014 was crippled and diminished by political in-fighting in Brussels. (Spain and Portugal insisted in being included too, despite the low incendiary levels in the Iberian Peninsula that year.)

Even the European Parliament, now made up of 1370 members, has broken itself up into regional chambers, meeting as a whole only in one, mostly ceremonial, plenary session a year (in an exhibition hall in Düsseldorf). Turnout at the last elections was 35 per cent. Only the Court of Justice tries to hold the ring for a single and indivisible Union, respecting the Treaty-based institutional system. But the Court seems to be suffocating under the weight of litigation, and cases take on average five years to be heard.

Needless to say, there is continuing pressure for further institutional reform and an almost endless intergovernmental conference tries to find formulae that will tighten the ties that bind. Driven to frustration by what is perceived as a failure of political leadership at the highest level in the Union, the political initiative has passed to the regions. Civil society is alive and well, refreshed in the West by the example of a vibrant democracy in the newer member states.

A new project for a federal constitution has been tabled, and has won the support of all seven Innsbruck states plus the UK, which is clearly beginning to tire of its self-exclusion. A new American President has also expressed support for a more united Europe.

The Committee of the Regions was disbanded in the Treaty of Warsaw (2006) and replaced by a new Council of the Regions to which only representatives of autonomous regional authorities are admitted. Led by the Basque, Catalan and Scottish Parliaments, the initiative soon caught on in the new member states. Poland, for example, quickly granted regional autonomy to Gdansk, Wroclaw and Cracow. Fears that the new EU Council of the Regions would be dominated by the German Länder proved unfounded as competitive city-regions emerged everywhere. In some instances, these regions began to be better connected with each other than with their own national capitals. Soon their external profile began to outstrip even that of the Commission — not least in environmental and humanitarian causes worldwide. The Council of the Regions also established effective partnerships with those few viable provinces in Russia that are doing something to compensate for the lack of the overall development of that country.

The economic performance of the European Union as a whole was more volatile than that of *Superstate Europa*, and regional diversity greater. But a gradual specialisation developed among the regions to mutual advantage. The automotive and shipbuilding industries moved East, while the European research effort was concentrated in the West. Mobility among skilled and professional workers has grown rapidly. Traditional agriculture (although now genetically modified) was concentrated in the Danube basin and in Southern Europe, while the more Northern states concentrated on afforestation, countryside management and organic products.

The European Union University, based in the former European Parliamentary premises at Strasbourg, has campuses in every member state and has established the norm for both undergraduate and postgraduate degree courses. A premier league of a dozen European universities compete with the best in the USA. The arts flourish, especially in the provinces, as the old national capitals experience something of a decline.

Global affairs are dominated by the USA and China. The Union plays a more modest but supportive role in reform of the international institutions, including the United Nations. Its one serious initiative — the Global Community for Sustainable Development — has attracted the active support of South Africa, India, Australasia, Argentina, Brazil and Chile, as well as Japan. Neither the Americans nor the Chinese participate.

The EU and NAFTA established a free trade zone as one of the consequences of the recession in 2008-09. APEC joined shortly afterwards.

A Pan-European Security and Cooperation Treaty was negotiated in the Euro-Atlantic Partnership Council, but critics doubt its viability in circumstances where the USA is still in a hegemonic position with regard to all other members. Turkey's recent accession has not exactly helped to enhance the cohesion of EU security strategy, but hostility to Turkish membership fell away once Ankara had withdrawn its troops from Northern Cyprus and granted regional autonomy for the Kurds in the South East. Istanbul, with 13 million inhabitants, is the largest metropolis in the EU.

SCENARIO 3: *EUROPE ADRIFT*

There are twenty-four members of the European Union — the present fifteen plus Poland, the Czech Republic, Hungary, the three Baltic states, Slovakia, Slovenia and Malta.

The Treaty of Nice was ratified in 2002, but there was no consequential agreement between member states on either the agenda or process of the next scheduled intergovernmental conference in 2004. As soon as Nice came into force, the Germans and Benelux proposed a raft of measures of 'closer cooperation' in the fields of social and fiscal policy. The UK rejected those proposals and began actively to recruit, with some success, the incoming candidate countries to support its own determinedly intergovernmentalist, anti-federalist approach.

Reform of the common agricultural policy was stymied as the new-comers, especially Poland, demanded equal treatment under the existing regime. The rising costs of the CAP made agreement on the review of the Union's financial perspectives after 2006 impossible, and a succession of emergency, supplementary budgets became the rule rather than the exception. Five years on, the European Investment Bank defaulted on its loan commitments.

When the accession negotiations got tough, the candidate countries threatened to restore ties with Moscow, including in the military field, thus putting the EU under great pressure from the US to make concessions.

Drawing the obvious conclusions, the Council agreed to lower the threshold for membership. The new states joined enjoying significant derogations from the acquis communautaire and, in some cases, such as migration of labour and protection of the environment, with transitional periods so long as to greatly weaken both the duties of membership and the privileges derived from it.

Of the other candidates, Switzerland aborted its accession negotiations when the proposed EU Charter of Fundamental Rights was not included in a constitutional treaty.

Turkey, whose own application had been blocked, threatened to disrupt Nato if Cyprus were admitted to the EU. The Baltic states were unable to maintain their progress towards integration after they were affected by deepening chaos in Russia, including the mutiny of the navy and the nuclear disaster at Murmansk (2006). Renewed fighting in the Balkans, particularly between Serbs and Albanians, caused the Union to suspend accession negotiations with all other candidates. The corrupt and bankrupt Turkish government annexes Northern Cyprus and launches a futile claim on Western Thrace. Insurrection broke out in Turkey, with armed leftists, Islamist fundamentalists and Kurdish separatists fighting each other as well as the Ankara regime.

Ensuing resentment at American interference in European affairs made it impossible for the EU leaders to take a positive line at the WTO talks. NGOs organised effective political opposition to EU connivance in further trade liberalisation, forming an unholy alliance with protectionist trade unions in Europe as well as in the USA. China remained outside the WTO.

On the fear of a slump in world trade, Wall Street investors withdrew support from new wave companies. In the 'Dot Com Crash' of 2004 the dollar lost 40 per cent of its value in two months. The euro managed to stabilise itself but the pound sterling, still dithering on the edge of membership of the single currency, followed the dollar sharply downwards. When the UK finally applied to join the euro in the middle of the currency crisis it was refused admission by the euro-zone members, led by France. In the resulting general election, the Tory party was returned with a huge majority on an anti-European ticket.

Prolonged economic recession ensued. Growth in the euro-zone over the decade averaged only 1.5 per cent; unemployment remained stubbornly high everywhere, and social unrest mushroomed. There remains no semblance of the European social model. The labour market is highly flexible, with immigrants hired and fired without social protection. The prison population increases fourfold — rivaling American proportions. Refugees and asylum seekers become the target of routine violence, and right-wing political parties thrive. Financial instability, leading to the collapse of credit institutions in the poorer regions, accentuated the sense of disaffection from the European project. 'More Europe' was associated in the public mind by a loss of control.

After a quarter of a century of fairly sustained liberalisation, mental, physical and technical barriers begin to go back up.

The European Commission begins to act more and more like a sub-committee of the Council. Its own administrative reforms faltered when faced with stiff opposition from the staff unions. Relations between the Commission and European Parliament became increasingly adversarial, and several Commissioners were forced to resign after circumstantial evidence emerged of fraud. While it struggles to maintain its regulatory functions, the Commission has almost ceased to initiate policy. Turnout in European Parliamentary elections falls to below 30 per cent, and the development of transnational political parties is reversed.

The European Council becomes involved in day-to-day decision making for the Union, much of it crisis management. As government authority faltered at EU and national level, competing city-regions begin to assert themselves. Many of these cities have radical mayors, elected by a population angered at rising criminality, pollution and congestion. Working together, these civic leaders try to compensate for the lack of cohesion and direction at the international level, thus providing one of the very few external manifestations of European integration. Several member states become almost dysfunctional. As the Kingdom of Belgium disintegrates, Brussels becomes a sovereign territory of the European Union.

The Nato members of the EU provide spasmodic assistance to American military missions, and the sole objective of EU foreign and security policy is not to provoke a US withdrawal from Europe at least until the prolonged civil war in the territory of the former USSR is over. The UN is largely impotent.

Popular hostility to European support for US policy grows, leading to violent demonstrations in every capital city and to the destabilisation of more than one administration. A media war develops between US and non-US owned newspapers and television companies, driving out competition and reducing further the pluralistic nature of European political debate. Political parties become associated with pro and anti-American ideology; few speak up for European unity. Overtly racist parties do well in elections.

Internal security becomes a preoccupation of the EU states. In Britain, France and Germany, the police have emergency powers to detain suspected illegal immigrants without trial. Italy and Spain suffer widespread terrorism from separatist and mafia forces, who in some instances join forces to combat state authority. Drug trafficking and addiction rises uncontrollably.

The Roman Catholic Church schisms. The reformists condone gay and married clergy, women priests and abortion. The embattled papacy declines as a moral force throughout the world. In Europe's universities, a new individualist, anti-authoritarian theology rises, with strong ecumenical tendencies.

The European Union's Charter of Fundamental Rights is revoked unilaterally by the Council. The disintegration of the Council of Europe is the ultimate provocation: latterly small groups begin to refresh federalist thought, often led by brilliant, innovative but frustrated and impoverished scientists.

SCENARIO 4: *FEDERAL UNION*

This fourth scenario takes the form of a constitution for a federal union of Europe. It compromises a preamble and just thirteen key articles. Its purpose is to make a future Union more democratic and efficient. Citizens of such a Union would have a better idea of how they are governed than they do now, and of how to participate in the transnational political system.

The constitution is based on the existing institutional structure and reflects the separation of powers inherent in the present European Union. But it raises the potency of what we have achieved already by several degrees in response to the driving forces we have analysed earlier.

Such a constitutional development would certainly be apt for Europe 2020, although there would be no reason to wait that long if the political will were to manifest itself beforehand. The constitutional debate, after all, has already begun.

A CONSTITUTION FOR 2020

Preamble

The states and citizens of the European Union,

Determined

    to live together in freedom, justice and peace,

    to uphold democracy and the rule of law,

    to guarantee fundamental rights to all the people in the Union,

    to respect the diverse cultures of Europe,

    to organise our relations together,

Do establish this as our Constitution.

Article 1 — membership

1. The European Union shall comprise its member states and citizens. The Union shall have legal personality.

2. The Union shall admit other states and their citizens according to the provisions of Article 12.

3. The Union may extend to any European state not being a member state of the Union any of the provisions of this Constitution; such states will be deemed to be associate members of the Union.

4. Member states may withdraw from the Union on terms to be agreed with the Union acting under the provisions of Article 12.

5. Membership rights of a member state may be revoked or reinstated on the initiative of the Commission or Court, with the approval of three-quarters of the member states in the Council and of three-quarters of the members of the European Parliament.

Article 2 — citizenship

1. All citizens of the member states are also citizens of the European Union.

2. Union citizens resident for a period of more than five years within a member state other than their own shall have the same rights and duties as citizens of that state.

3. The Charter of Fundamental Rights of the Union is part of the basic law of the Union and is annexed to this constitution. It is binding upon the institutions and agencies of the European Union. It is binding upon member states and their subsidiary authorities when and in so far as they implement Union law and policy.

Article 3 — objectives

1. The Union shall set itself the following objectives:

   to promote economic and social progress;

   to enhance the environment of the Union and the world;

   to establish the free movement of goods, persons, capital and services;

   to secure and defend the Union.

2. The Union shall fulfil its objectives in a manner demonstrating consistency and solidarity.

Article 4 — competence & subsidiarity

1. The European Union shall act only in accordance with this Constitution. Its actions shall not go beyond what is necessary to achieve its objectives. Its decisions will be taken as closely as possible to the citizen without impairing the effective operation of the Union.

2. The Union shall have the exclusive power to make laws in accordance with its principles and in pursuit of its objectives as laid down in this Constitution relating to:

   - internal and external trade,

   - currency and monetary policy,

   - Union taxation and expenditure not exceeding seven per cent of gross domestic product,

   - asylum and immigration,

   - environmental matters of concern to more than one member state.

3. The Treaties of the European Union and all laws enacted under them shall be laws of the Union save where they are inconsistent with this Constitution.

4. The constitutions and laws of the member states shall apply save where they are inconsistent with this Constitution.

Article 5 — legislature

1. The legislative and budgetary powers of the Union shall be vested in the European Parliament and the Council, each of which shall be responsible for its own working arrangements.

2. The Parliament shall comprise 770 members elected for a five-year term by the citizens of the Union by direct universal suffrage according to proportional representation. 700 members shall be elected in regional constituencies. 70 members shall be elected from across the territory of the Union.

3. The Parliament shall act by a simple majority except where this Constitution otherwise provides.

4. The Council shall comprise representatives of the member states. The Council shall act by a qualified majority except where this Constitution otherwise provides. The qualified majority shall be made up of a majority of member states representing a majority of the population of the Union. The Council shall be chaired by the President of the Commission or his or her representative.

5. A draft law or budget shall be enacted when approved by both the Parliament and the Council.

Article 6 — judiciary

1. The European Court of Justice shall be the Supreme Court of the European Union. The Court shall be responsible for its own working arrangements.

2. The judges of the Court of Justice, chosen from jurists whose qualifications and independence are beyond doubt, shall be appointed by the Council and the Parliament, acting by a majority of its members, for a non-renewable period of nine years.

3. The Court of Justice shall ensure that, in the interpretation and application of this Constitution and of legislation enacted under it, the law is observed.

Article 7 — heads of government

1. The European Council shall comprise the head of state or government of each member state together with the President of the European Commission.

2. The European Council shall nominate the President of the Commission and shall issue general political guidelines for the Union.

3. Meetings of the European Council will be chaired by one of their number by rotation for a period of six months.

Article 8 — executive

1. After nomination by the European Council, the President of the Commission shall be approved by the Parliament, acting by a majority of its members.

2. There shall be nine other members of the Commission who shall be nominated by the President in accord with the Council and approved by the Parliament.

3. The Commission shall initiate legislation, execute the laws, manage the implementation of policy, control expenditure and negotiate treaties on behalf of the Union. It shall be responsible for its own working arrangements.

4. The Commission shall serve for a five-year term unless dismissed by a two-thirds majority of the members of the Parliament in which case a new Commission shall be appointed for the rest of the term.

Article 9 — consultation

1. There shall be a Committee of the Regions comprised of representatives of those regions enjoying both administrative and legislative autonomy within their member states.

2. There shall be an Economic and Social Committee comprised of representatives of the social partners and of civil society.

3. These Committees shall be consulted by the Commission before it initiates a legislative act. They shall assist the Commission, Council and Parliament in the review of Union law and policy.

Article 10 — financial institutions

1. The European Central Bank shall manage the currency of the Union according to monetary policy guidelines established jointly by the Commission, Council and the Parliament. The governors of the Central Bank, chosen from persons of proven financial experience whose independence is beyond doubt, shall be appointed by the Council and the Parliament, acting by a majority of its members, for a non-renewable period of seven years.

2. The European Court of Auditors shall be responsible for the audit. The members of the Court of Auditors, chosen from accountants of proven experience and whose independence is beyond doubt, shall be appointed by the Council and the Parliament, acting by a majority of its members, for a period of six years.

Article 11 — law-making

1. There shall be a hierarchy of acts comprising (a) regulations, which shall have general application and be binding in entirety and directly applicable, (b) directives, which shall be binding as to the result to be achieved but shall leave to member state authorities the choice and form of methods, and (c) executive decisions, which the Commission shall determine.

2. On the initiative of the Commission, the choice of legislative and executive act shall be taken jointly by the Council and Parliament according to an inter-institutional agreement to be approved by the Council acting by qualified majority and by a two-thirds majority of the members of the Parliament.

Article 12 — amendments

1. Amendments to this Constitution may be proposed by the European Parliament or any member state and shall take effect either

> if supported by a two-thirds majority of the members of the Parliament and by the Council, acting unanimously, and ratified by member states according to their own constitutional requirements;

> or

> if supported by a two-thirds majority of the members of the Parliament and by a majority of the citizens of the Union voting in a referendum and ratified by the Council.

2. Amendments to this Constitution or to the Charter of Fundamental Rights shall be drafted by a Convention. The Convention shall represent the European Council, Commission, Parliament and member state parliaments. There shall be consensus among the four parties to the Convention.

Article 13 — entry into force

1. This Constitution shall enter into force once it has been approved by the European Council, by a two-thirds majority of the members of the Parliament and by a majority of the citizens of the existing Union voting in a referendum,

or

ratified by all the member states of the Union according to their own constitutional requirements, with the assent of the European Parliament.

2. Any member state deciding not to adopt this Constitution may seek associate membership as Article 1.3 provides.

NOTES

[1] The authors are particularly grateful to Richard Blackman and John Pinder for their help with this project.

[2] This fascinating fact is drawn from a recent OECD Report, *The Future of the Global Economy; Towards a Long Boom?*, Paris, OECD, 1999.

[3] For the development of this idea, see John Pinder, 'The Rule of Law for a Uniting World: a global community for sustainable development,' in W.J.M. van Genugten et al. (eds), *Realism and Moralism in International Relations*, Kluwer Law International, 1999.

[4] See Andrew Duff, 'Towards a European Federal Society' in Kim Feus, ed., *The EU Charter of Fundamental Rights: text and commentaries*, with an introduction by Lord Lester of Herne Hill QC, Federal Trust, 2000.

[5] For a useful discussion of these issues, see John Plender, *Bigger companies, smaller governments — power and responsibility in the global economy*, London, Lloyds TSB Forum 2000.

[6] *Europe's Future: Four Scenarios*, London, Federal Trust, 1991.

[7] The 1996 Chatham House Forum Report, *Unsettled Times: three stony paths to 2015*, London, Royal Institute of International Affairs, 1996.

[8] Michael Emerson, *Redrawing the Map of Europe*, London, Macmillan, 1998.

[9] *Europe Beyond the Millennium - Making Sense of Tomorrow*, Andersen Consulting, 1998.

[10] H.H.J. Labohm, J.Q.Th. Rood and A. van Staden, *'Europe' on the Threshold of the 21st Century: Five Scenarios*, The Hague, Clingendael-Study, December 1998.

[11] *Waving or Drowning? Four Scenarios for New Europe to 2010*, PricewaterhouseCoopers, 2000.

[12] Gilles Bertrand (coordinator), Anne Michalski and Lucio R. Pench, *Scenarios Europe 2010: Five Possible Futures for Europe*, Brussels, European Commission, Forward Studies Unit, Working Paper, July 1999. For an earlier study from the Commission, see Alexis Jacquemin and David Wright, eds, *The European Challenges Post-1992: Shaping Factors, Shaping Actors*, London, Edward Elgar, 1993.